THE
KU KLUX KLAN
IN WOOD COUNTY, OHIO

THE
KU KLUX KLAN
IN WOOD COUNTY, OHIO

MICHAEL E. BROOKS

Charleston · London

THE
History
PRESS

Published by The History Press
Charleston, SC 29403
www.historypress.net

Copyright © 2014 by Michael E. Brooks
All rights reserved

First published 2014

Manufactured in the United States

ISBN 978.1.62619.334.5

Library of Congress CIP data applied for.

CONTENTS

PREFACE

A s any author will attest, writing a book is an arduous process that requires the assistance of many people to make the work successful. Among the people playing important roles in this book was my research assistant, Chloe Koscheva-Scissons. Chloe spent many hours poring through hundreds of copies of archived newspapers and other documents in her efforts to help me examine the rise and fall of the Ku Klux Klan in Wood County. Without Chloe's tireless efforts and useful suggestions, this book would not have been possible.

Thanks also to the editors at The History Press for accepting the book proposal and seeing it through the production and marketing stages. This is a talented group of publishing professionals who provided me with a great deal of knowledge of the industry.

The folks at the Center for Archival Collections at Bowling Green State University were extremely helpful during the time I spent in the archives. Thanks to Steve Charter, Marilyn Levinson, Samantha Ashby, Libby Hertenstein and everyone else at the CAC who ran back and forth to locate materials I needed. Thanks also to the staff at the Wood County Historical Society, especially Dana Nemeth, Holly Hartlerode Uppal and Mike McMaster.

Many thanks to the following colleagues who provided insightful comments on drafts of this book: Michael Carver, Amílcar Challú, Rex Childers, Douglas Forsyth, Benjamin Greene, Beth Griech-Polelle, Walter Grunden, Ruth Herndon, Nicole Jackson, Rebecca Mancuso, Scott Martin, Dustin McLoughlin, Ian Mladjov, Apollos Nwauwa and Tina Thomas.

PREFACE

Special thanks goes to Tony DeIuliis, who discovered in the mid-1970s the cache of Wood County Klan documents that was critical to the research for this book. His understanding of the importance of these materials, plus his persistence in getting archivists interested in preserving them, deserves recognition, and I hope that this book lives up to Tony's vision for what might be possible with these KKK documents.

My deepest debt of gratitude goes to my wife, Kimberlyn, who encouraged me to return and restart my academic career after a long hiatus. She patiently provided support throughout my undergraduate and graduate years, helped me transcribe source material for this book and offered a number of thoughtful suggestions on the manuscript that seemed to be the exact advice I needed at the moment.

Finally, the general topic of white supremacy can be something of a minefield for researchers as for many people, wounds from the civil rights struggles of the second half of the twentieth century are still fresh. In my research and writing, I have uncovered a great deal of archival information that by twenty-first-century standards would be considered strongly offensive. For the purposes of historical accuracy, I have elected not to censor any of the historical sources to spare sensitive readers. Keep in mind that in a contextual sense, the racist language used in the primary sources referenced in this book was considered "normal" for the time period.

In addition, the emergence of the Internet has provided white supremacists, neo-Nazis and white nationalists a particularly powerful recruiting and broadcasting tool since the mid-1990s, and there has been a growth of activity by such groups. In some ways, racial tensions have increased in the past decade due to the unlimited exposure that hate groups can generate via electronic media and the resultant backlash by concerned citizens. Thus, my apologies to those who might be offended by the words and deeds of historical actors, but often history is not pretty. Sometimes it can be downright ugly.

INTRODUCTION

T he choir and congregation had just finished singing a hymn entitled "The Path of the Just" during an evening service when a group of nine men wearing Ku Klux Klan robes marched into the church. One of the Klan members carried the American flag, while another Kluxer held high a copy of the Bible as the anonymous men entered the house of worship.[1]

The hooded visitors, parading in formation, continued up the aisle to the altar, where they presented the minister with an introductory letter and a financial contribution to the church.

The Klan group then turned and faced the audience, at which point one of the Klansmen opened the Bible and began reading from the twelfth chapter of the New Testament book of Romans:

> *Therefore, I urge you, brothers and sisters, in view of God's mercy, to offer your bodies as a living sacrifice, holy and pleasing to God—this is your true and proper worship. Do not conform to the pattern of this world, but be transformed by the renewing of your mind. Then you will be able to test and approve what God's will is—his good, pleasing and perfect will.*

The Klan members then directed the congregation to kneel in prayer, at which point, one of the Kluxers led the assembled church members in the Lord's Prayer. After this impromptu KKK ceremony, the hooded members of the Klan silently marched out of the church and into the chilly February evening air.

This scene likely seems surreal enough to a twenty-first-century reader who is decades removed from the point in time when the Ku Klux Klan was a powerful organization with millions of members. Even stranger, however, is the fact that the above Klan activity took place on February 11, 1923, in the city of Bowling Green, Ohio, at the local United Brethren Church. This event took place not in the Deep South of the Jim Crow era or the height of the civil rights movement in the 1960s, but in a rather sleepy midwestern college town.

The Klan visit to the United Brethren Church was hardly the "surprise" described by the newspaper reporter for the *Wood County Republican* in its coverage of the event. Word had leaked out prior to the Ku Klux Klan event, as the main auditorium filled and adjacent classrooms had to be opened to accommodate the hundreds of additional visitors that the Klan event attracted.

Most importantly, the Reverend Rush A. Powell, minister of the United Brethren Church, was himself a charter member of the Wood County Chapter of the Knights of the Ku Klux Klan.

Reverend Powell welcomed the Klan to Trinity United Brethren Church with open arms, telling the congregation that he "stood for the same principles"[2] as those held by his hooded guests. After the Klan Bible reading and prayer, Reverend Powell spoke of the perils the United States faced with criminal activity, undesirable immigrants and a general decline in morality. While not publicly declaring himself a Klan member, Reverend Powell assured his audience that the Klan was formed to address those threats to America.

It is tempting to write off events such as this Klan visit as aberrations in an otherwise forward movement of American history toward greater tolerance and a more inclusive society. Yet Reverend Rush A. Powell was but one of millions of faces of the Ku Klux Klan that emerged in the early twentieth century, and Ohio's Wood County proved to be a bastion of Klan activity for a lengthy period of time. The Klan, instead of being a fleeting historical anomaly, represented a highly visible face of widespread American intolerance and bigotry.

The Ku Klux Klan took root in Wood County and maintained a significant presence for at least two decades. Its legacy can still be discerned nearly a century after the Klan officially appeared on the landscape of this otherwise quiet, agriculture-dominated region in Northwest Ohio.

This book examines the rise and fall of the Ku Klux Klan in Wood County, Ohio, an area located in a heavily agricultural region in the northwestern corner of the state. The Wood County klavern was one of thousands of

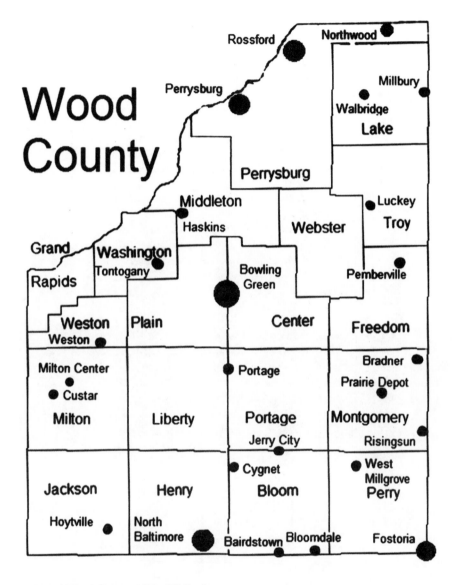

Map of Wood County. *Michael E. Brooks.*

chapters of the Klan that sprang up during the 1920s in the era of the so-called Second Klan, when membership in the organization numbered in the millions in the United States.

We are fortunate that important records of the Wood County Ku Klux Klan Chapter 107 have survived into the twenty-first century. Given the

Sample page of the Wood County Ku Klux Klan membership ledger. *Center for Archival Collections.*

secretive nature of the organization, detailed membership records of local Klan chapters are somewhat rare, but the Wood County Klan is an exception to that tendency. The core of the research for this book is based on careful study of the meticulous membership and dues registers that Klan officials maintained.

Klan members provided the local chapter with a range of personal information, including names, home addresses, employment information and the name of the person who referred the individual to the group.

Klan officials recorded dates of initiation, payment of dues and additional information on banishment, departure or death of the member.

Klan records also contain interesting notes in the margins and unfilled columns of dues, registers and membership files, such as the case of a Klan member banished in 1925. A margin note provided a clue for the banishment: "MARRIED CATHOLIC."

Other notes included details about Klan members who transferred from (or to) other Klan chapters, members suspended for nonpayment of dues, members who faced financial difficulties, members who received Klan funeral ceremonies or members who moved without leaving forwarding addresses.

Klan membership and dues records were crosschecked against other sources from the time period. These additional sources included census rolls, city directories, newspaper articles, birth and death records and

Sample Klan membership card. Center for Archival Collections.

church membership lists. After assembling the database of names and relevant information, analysis of the data was conducted to develop general characteristics of the typical member of the Wood County Ku Klux Klan.

Far from being a temporary aberration, the emergence of the Ku Klux Klan in Wood County was in some ways normal for the American Midwest of the 1920s. However, the Wood County klavern of the Klan exhibited its own distinctive characteristics, and Klan leaders in the county carefully tailored the group's message to local and regional concerns.

The Klan in many ways found a ready-made audience in Wood County for its ideologies of racism, nativism and religious intolerance. While the national recruitment and organization personnel of the Ku Klux Klan helped plant the seeds for the group's emergence in Wood County, the Klan also benefited from the fertile ground of preexisting racial, religious and political views among many county residents.

UNDERSTANDING
WOOD COUNTY

Winn Stein looked out his front door and saw a group of approximately twenty angry men armed with shotguns assembled on his property. Stein happened to be up and around after midnight on the morning of May 9, 1922, because he and his family were rousted out of bed by the sound of shotgun fire and breaking glass as the mob finished shooting out sixteen windows in the Stein residence.

The reason for the late-night attack was the fact that Stein and his family gave shelter to Otto P. Tracy, the former principal of the Walbridge elementary school who faced criminal charges of sexual activity with students at the school.[3]

Stein telephoned the county sheriff and then addressed the mob, asking their purpose for the violent "visit." A spokesman for the armed vigilantes insisted that they "wanted Tracy delivered to them." After informing the mob that the sheriff had been summoned, the armed men disappeared into the night.[4]

The vigilante attack underscored a feature of life in Wood County in the 1920s: citizens were prepared to take matters into their own hands if they believed that the legal system was not working as they thought it should.

While Wood County in the early twentieth century was hardly a lawless place akin to the Wild West, the limited law enforcement resources in the sparsely populated county meant that citizens sometimes took it on themselves to deliver what they perceived to be justice. Sometimes scores were settled using fists and guns instead of calling the police, and every once

Unidentified men at Cygnet, Ohio, with weapons collection. *Center for Archival Collections.*

in a while, a dead body would turn up in the countryside about which few questions would be asked by authorities.

Most of Wood County was once covered by the Great Black Swamp, a 40- by 120-mile stretch of wetlands that seemed almost impenetrable to early colonists. Due to the pervasiveness of the Great Black Swamp, the first roads consisted of logs placed perpendicular to the flow of traffic, so-called corduroy roads. The presence of malaria-carrying mosquitoes also limited settlement and development, as the area was long noted for being an unhealthy region where travelers and new settlers might quickly succumb to what was known as "fever and ague" (the phrase refers to the alternating high fever and shaking chills associated with a malaria attack).

Settlement, growth and development of the county thus faced significant environmental hurdles that were not solved until the eventual draining of the Great Black Swamp in the second half of the nineteenth century. As the swamp began to be drained, fertile croplands opened up to farmers.

Wood County was among the administrative divisions created by the state of Ohio after a series of treaties with Native American groups who once lived in the region. The state legislature officially recognized Wood County

A home in a swampy area, Wood County. *Center for Archival Collections.*

on February 20, 1820. Wood County once stretched north to the border of the state of Michigan, but its northern boundaries were redrawn at the Maumee River when Lucas County was carved out of the northern half of Wood County in 1835.

The Maumee River serves as a geographical boundary between Wood County and most of Lucas County to the north. To a lesser extent, the Maumee River has also emerged as something of a cultural boundary between the more urbanized Lucas County and the more rural Wood County. During the 1920s, connections across the Maumee were limited to a few bridges, rail lines and interurban rail lines.

Wood County even today is largely rural (with the exception of urban pockets in Bowling Green and the extreme northern cities of the county), and agriculture still plays an important role in the local economy in the twenty-first century. The Ohio Department of Agriculture estimated in 2012 that over 81 percent of the total acreage in the county consists of farmland being actively cultivated.[5]

Grains, soybeans, fruits and vegetables make up the vast majority of agricultural products in Wood County in the early twenty-first century.

The county today ranks first among the eighty-eight counties in the state in soybean and wheat production and second in the state in corn production as measured in bushels.[6] The total value of agriculture in Wood County in 2007 was over $125 million,[7] and Wood County has long been one of the leading centers of agriculture in the state of Ohio.

In keeping with its agriculture-related tradition and culture, Wood County today is home to the National Tractor Pullers Association (NTPA) championship each year at the Wood County Fairgrounds. For the event, thousands of tractor-pull fans flock to Wood County, and the fairgrounds transform into "Pulltown."

At the beginning of the twentieth century, agriculture was an even larger component of the county's economy. The *Farm Journal Rural Directory* reported in 1916 that "91 percent of the area of the county is in its farms." At that time, there were a total of 4,357 farms in the county, and around 60 percent of the farms in Wood County were "operated by their owners." Corn was the leading agricultural product of the county at that time, followed by oats, wheat and potatoes.[8]

Wood County also once boasted flourishing petroleum and natural gas industries. The southern half of the county in particular was noted for the discovery of significant oil and gas wells in the late nineteenth and early twentieth centuries.

Photograph of Hocking Valley train in front of an oil derrick, 1920. *Center for Archival Collections.*

By the beginning of the 1920s, however, the boom period for Wood County in energy extraction had started to wane, and production of these energy sources entered a period of significant decline. This contributed to a general feeling of economic uncertainty in the county, and many of the several thousand workers in the county's oil and natural gas industries would eventually become unemployed or forced to find work in other industries.

DEMOGRAPHICS OF WOOD COUNTY

Slightly less than half of the total population of the county today can be found in two cities: Perrysburg and Bowling Green. There has been a gradual population shift in the county away from rural areas and into the larger cities. Bowling Green and Perrysburg represented only 18 percent of the county's total population at the time of the census in 1920.

Bowling Green is the current county seat, and the two cities are located about 13 miles apart on Ohio's State Route 25. Bowling Green in the twenty-first century still possesses more of a small town character, while also boasting the presence of a state university.

Meanwhile, Perrysburg features a significantly larger number of upscale neighborhoods and shopping centers, and the municipality is one of the major suburbs of the city of Toledo. Historically, the city of Perrysburg has also been consistently oriented more toward the Toledo metropolitan area than many of the other Wood County communities.

While Bowling Green and Perrysburg are friendly rivals today, the two cities were for a period of time somewhat bitter adversaries. This was especially the case during the period when the state of Ohio in 1868 moved the county seat from Perrysburg to Bowling Green.[9] One account described the conflict over the location of the county seat as "intense" and that there was "bitter denunciation on both sides."[10]

During the 1920s, the city of Bowling Green was about twice the size of Perrysburg in total population. This disparity was even greater when taking into account the roughly two thousand college students attending Bowling Green Normal College each year of the decade. (Today, this is Bowling Green State University.)[11] Until the census of 1940, guidelines for census-takers stipulated that the parental address, not the college address, was the residence where students should be documented by census workers.

THE KU KLUX KLAN IN WOOD COUNTY, OHIO

The demographic and financial center of the southern end of the county is the village of North Baltimore, and around 3,400 people resided in the village as of the 2010 census. North Baltimore was once a boomtown with significant wealth during the oil boom of the late nineteenth and early twentieth centuries, but the eventual depletion of oil and natural gas reserves brought to a close the village's brief flirtation with regional prominence.

While there has gradually emerged greater ethnic and racial diversity in Wood County over the past several decades, the county remains overwhelmingly white. The areas with the greatest demographic diversity are areas on and around the state university in Bowling Green, plus the northern Wood County cities of Perrysburg, Rossford and Northwood, which are as much suburbs of the city of Toledo as they are representative of the demographics of Wood County. The Census Bureau estimated for 2012 that over 93 percent of the county was white, with African Americans, Asian Americans and Latinos combining for a little more than 5 percent of the county's population.[12]

During the 1920s, the county consisted almost exclusively of white residents. The 1920 census recorded only 248 African Americans in the county, along with 37 biracial residents (people who were described on the census forms as "mulatto"). Residents categorized as white thus constituted 99.37 percent of the population of Wood County.

Contemporary residents of Wood County were aware of the relative lack of racial and ethnic diversity in the area. The 1916 county directory proudly reported that "the farm population of Wood County is almost exclusively native-born white." Moreover, noted the directory, there were "but few foreign, and only one negro farmer in the entire county."[13]

The location of African American and biracial residents is of interest in the study of Klan activity in the county. Nearly 95 percent of persons of color who were residents of the county lived in its extreme northern areas (present-day Perrysburg, Rossford and Northwood). The remaining persons of color were mostly limited to a few dozen residents of the city of Bowling Green. Most of the smaller villages in Wood County during the 1920s were exclusively white.

Most of the residents of Wood County in the 1920s were at least second-generation Americans. During the nineteenth century, the vast majority of immigrants who settled in Wood County were native German speakers, and these immigrants principally arrived between 1840 and 1890.

During the late nineteenth and early twentieth centuries, though, there was a shift in the countries of origin of immigrants who arrived in Wood

TABLE 1
Wood County Demographic Statistics by Municipality
and Census Racial Designation

MUNICIPALITY	TOTAL	WHITE	BLACK	BIRACIAL
Bowling Green	5,788	5,758	17	13
Ross Township	4,184	3,986	190	8
North Baltimore	2,438	2,436	2	0
Perrysburg	2,429	2,400	22	7
Pemberville	938	938	0	0
Weston	844	844	0	0
Bradner	785	785	0	0
Tontogany	603	603	0	0
Prairie Depot	578	578	0	0
Walbridge	532	532	0	0
Cygnet	521	521	0	0
Grand Rapids	517	517	0	0
Bloomdale	509	509	0	0
Risingsun	477	477	0	0
Haskins	427	427	0	0
Hoytville	367	367	0	0
Custar	316	316	0	0
Portage	303	303	0	0
Jerry City	266	261	0	5
Luckey	249	249	0	0
Millbury	226	220	6	0
Milton Center	194	194	0	0

County. Most of the county continued to consist of native-born residents and a small number of German-speaking immigrants, but a few areas in northern Wood County began to attract large numbers of immigrants from southern and Eastern Europe.

The 1920 census indicated that there were about two thousand residents of Wood County who were foreign born, representing less than 5 percent of the total population. Many towns and villages attracted very few southern and Eastern European immigrants, but two areas in particular emerged as destinations for immigrants from these regions.

In 1920, the foreign-born population of Ross Township was nearly one-third of the township's total population. The area's manufacturing and

TABLE 2
Wood County Immigration Statistics by Municipality

MUNICIPALITY	TOTAL	FOREIGN-BORN	PERCENTAGE
Ross Township	4,184	1,277	30.52
Cygnet	521	54	10.36
Bairdstown	158	14	8.86
Pemberville	938	82	8.74
Walbridge	532	44	8.27
Luckey	249	18	7.23
Milton Center	194	12	6.19
Custar	316	19	6.01
Millbury	226	13	5.75
Perrysburg	2,429	124	5.10
Haskins	427	17	3.98
North Baltimore	2,438	87	3.57
Bowling Green	5,788	191	3.30
Bradner	785	22	2.80
Hoytville	367	10	2.72
Portage	303	8	2.64
Grand Rapids	517	13	2.51
Weston	844	21	2.49
Prairie Depot	578	14	2.42
Risingsun	477	9	1.89
Tontogany	603	11	1.82
Bloomdale	509	6	1.18
Jerry City	266	2	0.75

commercial enterprises offered employment opportunities to unskilled and low-skilled workers, and immigrants from such countries as Hungary, Belgium, Bulgaria, Greece, Italy, Poland, Croatia and Russia flocked to Ross Township in search of work. Over 60 percent of the immigrants in Wood County in 1920 lived in Ross Township.

Oil-drilling operations also served as magnets for the newer immigrant groups who settled in Wood County. This was especially true in towns that grew during Wood County's short-lived oil boom, such as Cygnet. Working on oil rigs was grueling and dangerous work, and employers were somewhat less concerned with ethnicity in making hiring decisions than many other area employers.

The heavy concentration of immigrants in just a few areas seems to have contributed to the hardened attitudes of native-born Wood County residents toward immigration, as the relative visibility of immigrants increased with these concentrated pockets of immigrant life. The village of Rossford in particular became the major focal point for the anger exhibited by nativists against newly arrived immigrants.

The issue of the perception of Rossford as a hotbed of illegal activity and moral decay was the subject of a 1924 *North Baltimore Times* editorial. Many Wood County residents, according to the editorial, saw Rossford as "a rendezvous of crooks, bootleggers, and undesirable foreigners" that was a "good place to stay away from." The negative perceptions about Rossford, the writer of the editorial claimed, were due to the "so-called 'Rossford crime wave' pictured by the Toledo and Bowling Green press." Readers of the paper were exposed only to the "the booze raids, the cutting scrapes of the foreigners, and the burglaries" instead of positive Rossford news.[14]

With regard to religious affiliation, persons identifying with Protestant denominations are the largest segment of the population of Wood County in the twenty-first century. The percentage of Wood County residents who attend a Catholic church is approximately 17.5 percent, which is about average for the state of Ohio, but the Catholic presence is much heavier in cities on the northern edge of the county such as Perrysburg and Rossford. In the early twentieth century, though, Wood County was heavily dominated by Protestant denominations, especially evangelical branches, and the influence of evangelical Protestants extended beyond religious spheres into culture and politics.

The Ohio Federation of Churches noted that in 1922 there were 117 different churches in Wood County, and these churches represented some 27 different denominations. The survey also noted that Wood County's Catholic population that year was about nine thousand people, translating into about 18 percent of the population. Protestant affiliation in the survey was nearly 75 percent of the county's residents.[15]

The Federation of Churches report also provided information about the number of clergy in Wood County. During the same period of 1921–22, there were fifty-six full-time clergy members and seventeen part-time members in the county to serve the religious needs of the population. A significant number of these seventy-three church officials would soon appear on the membership rolls of the Wood County chapter of the Knights of the Ku Klux Klan.

As an indicator of the power of churches in the lives of Wood County residents, the Ohio Federation of Churches report noted that ten of eighteen communities with populations under one thousand people had four or more churches each. The towns of Bloomdale and Walbridge each supported six churches despite the fact that these municipalities contained less than one thousand residents.[16] In fact, one of the principal recommendations of the report was that Wood County would benefit from an effort to consolidate churches, resulting in greater efficiency and the ability for each congregation to have its own minister.

ECONOMIC CONDITIONS IN WOOD COUNTY IN THE 1920S

The 1920s, at least prior to the stock market crash of 1929, is popularly known as the Roaring Twenties due to a lengthy period of sustained economic growth, especially in sectors such as consumer goods and construction. The annual growth rates in gross domestic product (GDP) in the United States were as high as 11 percent in the middle of the 1920s.

The spectacular growth in personal incomes experienced by some Americans in the middle of the 1920s, however, was not mirrored in many American counties that were more rural and dependent on agriculture for economic activity. Wood County certainly fell into this category of agriculture-dominated regions, and news accounts in the county during the 1920s exhibited a near-constant concern about the weak agricultural sector.

For many residents of Wood County, the 1920s was a time economic uncertainty. The depression of 1920–21 stubbornly persisted months after

Farmers cutting grain in Wood County. *Center for Archival Collections.*

recovery had begun to occur in many other parts of the United States. Agricultural producers in Wood County especially bore the brunt of the tough times, experiencing falling prices for agricultural commodities and decreases in land values.

An economist in 1924 observed that falling farm incomes and rising taxes were a deadly spiral for Ohio farmers. In layman's terms, "it required over twice as many hogs or beef cattle, two and a half times as much corn, or a half more than the prewar amount of butter to pay the taxes."[17]

Life for industrial workers in Wood County was similarly difficult. Wages fell during the depression in the first part of the decade, and incomes were slow to recover. Business owners and political leaders were staunchly anti-union, and it would be decades before organized labor made any significant inroads into improving the economic fortunes of industrial workers.

This economic uncertainty—as evidenced by historically high unemployment rates, declining farm incomes and sluggish postwar economic growth—was one of the most important factors in the rise of the reborn Ku Klux Klan in Ohio during the 1920s. Concerns about the economy were regularly expressed in news stories and editorials in local and county newspapers throughout the years of the Klan's peak influence.

In addition, newspapers frequently contained articles and editorials that warned of a coming economic catastrophe. This apocalyptic fear of impending financial doom was an emotion that Klan organizers would

Oil derrick in southern Wood County. *Center for Archival Collections.*

exploit in their recruiting efforts, especially among farmers, agricultural laborers and workers in industries like energy extraction.

The *Wood County Republican* captured many of these concerns in a 1924 article on the plight of farmers in Northwest Ohio. In addition to the flat or declining prices at which farmers could sell agricultural products, there were burdensome price hikes for most of the machinery and materials that Wood County farmers regularly purchased. Farmers were "hard-pressed to make a living" with the cost increases.[18]

In addition, local newspapers noted the increasing participation by farmers of Wood County in the political process. A 1920 editorial in the *Perrysburg Journal* commended area farmers for demonstrating "clear, incisive, earnest thought" that was "marked by loyal Americanism," adding that farmers in Wood County were "involved in solving political, social, and economic problems" to a greater extent than ever before.[19]

It was into this troubled economy and energetic political process that the Ku Klux Klan interjected itself, and Klan organizers effectively tapped into economic discontent in their efforts to rapidly expand the power of the Klan in Wood County.

2

THE RISE OF THE SECOND
KU KLUX KLAN

The Wood County Ku Klux Klan "held sway in Bowling Green" on the night of October 4, 1923. The group drew between "fifteen and twenty thousand people" to a KKK recruitment event, according to a report by the *Daily Sentinel-Tribune*. The KKK parade, which contained several marching bands and Klansmen on horses, "stretched out over a distance of a half a mile" in length.[20]

A fireworks extravaganza and the burning of "four huge crosses" brought the "mammoth meeting to a close." The *Sentinel-Tribune* reporter estimated the center cross to be over "forty feet high," and the reporter carefully detailed his estimation that "some 17,900 people" filled the Wood County Fairgrounds.[21]

To provide perspective, the crowd attending the Klan event represented a mass of people about two-fifths the size of the entire population of Wood County at the time. While at least half of the attendees were from surrounding counties, to the objective viewers on the ground, this was an unprecedented political event. How, then, did a relatively small Ohio farming region become such a major center of Klan activity in the 1920s?

A 1923 Ku Klux Klan parade. *Ohio Historical Society.*

A BRIEF HISTORY OF THE KU KLUX KLAN

The history of the Ku Klux Klan is typically divided by scholars into three distinct phases, each with unique characteristics and areas of focus. The first phase of the Klan is associated with the political violence that took place in the South in response to Reconstruction, running from roughly 1865 to 1874. The Klan's second phase generally dates from 1915 to the end of the Second World War, while the third phase of the Klan emerges during the height of the American civil rights movement in the 1950s and 1960s through the present day.[22]

The first Ku Klux Klan is the terror-based vigilante organization that emerged in the South after the Civil War. These were loosely connected bands of insurgents who used political violence to oppose what they viewed as northern infringement on southern political rights.

The origin of the name "Ku Klux Klan" is somewhat murky. The founders of the first wave of the Klan blended the Greek word *kuklos* ("circle") with "Klan" to create the alliterative name. A number of the group's rituals share similarities with Kuklos Adelphon, which was a southern college fraternity that operated in the decades before the Civil War. The fraternity had faded in popularity by midcentury, and by the 1870s, Kuklos Adelphon had ceased to exit.[23]

Typically, this first wave of Klan activity targeted politically active African Americans and white Republicans who sought to reshape the South during Reconstruction. While the formal structure of the first Klan was broken in the 1870s, lynchings and other violence by individuals sympathetic to the philosophies of the Ku Klux Klan continued up to the end of the nineteenth century. Groups such as the Red Shirts and the White League carried on the tradition of political violence that the first Klan unleashed. Over the course of the first phase of the Klan and its successor organizations, several thousand people were murdered by members or affiliates of—or individuals in sync with—the Invisible Empire.

The Ku Klux Klan reemerged in the early twentieth century, in part due to sympathetic portrayals of the KKK in books and other media. Of particular importance in the rebirth of the Klan was *Birth of a Nation*, the 1915 film by D.W. Griffiths that was based on a 1905 novel by Thomas F. Dixon Jr. entitled *The Clansman: An Historical Romance of the Ku Klux Klan*. In the film, Griffiths portrayed African Americans as lazy, drunken and oversexed buffoons. Conversely, the film depicted the Klan as a heroic group simply trying to restore order and morality in the post–Civil War South.

More than any other single factor, the film *Birth of a Nation* solidified the public image of the Ku Klux Klan as a bastion of morality and virtue, regardless of the unpleasant realities surrounding this terror-oriented group and its history of violence and intimidation. Tens of millions of Americans watched the film in the years after its release, giving a wide audience to this work of pro-Klan propaganda.

The creation of the second phase of the KKK was largely

Poster of the film *The Birth of a Nation*. *Author's collection.*

the brainchild of William Joseph Simmons, an Atlanta man who bounced around in a variety of careers before finding some financial success as a field organizer for fraternal organizations like the Woodsmen of the World. Simmons found inspiration for his revived version of the Ku Klux Klan in *Birth of a Nation*, and he also found useful for recruitment efforts the mob lynching of Leo Frank, a Jewish man convicted of murdering a thirteen-year-old girl. Frank's killers, who included many prominent political leaders, abducted him from a jail in Marietta and drove nearly seven hours across back roads in Georgia before hanging the man in the town of Milledgeville.[24]

The initial Klan group that Simmons formed included a few members of the Leo Frank lynch mob as well as two elderly men who claimed to be members of the first Ku Klux Klan. As part of their formation rituals, and also to generate publicity for the new Klan, the group climbed Stone Mountain and burned a large cross that was visible for several miles.

The group that Simmons formed grew slowly, numbering just a few thousand members by 1920. The second Klan under the direction of Simmons remained largely confined to the areas around Atlanta. Simmons hired a pair of public relations specialists, Elizabeth Tyler and Edward Young Clarke, to boost the group's membership. The Southern Publicity Association—the firm owned by Tyler and Clarke—produced immediate results for the Klan, and membership in the Klan skyrocketed.

The rebirth of the Ku Klux Klan in the early twentieth century was as much a business success as it was a social, cultural and political phenomenon. The Klan under the direction of Tyler and Clarke adopted an incentivized business model in which recruiters—known as kleagles at the local level—were paid a sizeable portion of the initiation fees of new members in exchange for their efforts to boost membership. From the $10.00 membership fee, $4.00 went to the kleagle when he signed a new member, $1.00 went to the King kleagle (regional recruitment leader), $0.50 went to the Grand Goblin (the state recruitment leader) and the remaining $4.50 was remitted to the national office in Atlanta.[25]

At its peak in the mid-1920s, the Ku Klux Klan boasted as many as 5 million members across the United States, and the group emerged as a powerful political force in many states. In Ohio, one of the Klan's strongest realms, membership likely peaked at over 300,000 Klansmen by 1925, and some estimates suggest that as many as 400,000 Ohioans had joined the Klan by mid-decade.[26]

Attacks by opponents of the Ku Klux Klan actually seemed to bolster the popularity of the group, at least temporarily. The period of the highest

THE RISE OF THE SECOND KU KLUX KLAN

Oil worker, oil derrick and cornfield in 1920. *Center for Archival Collections.*

membership growth appeared after a 1921 *New York World* exposé on Klan activities that prompted a 1922 congressional investigation of the Klan. Instead of derailing the growth of the Ku Klux Klan, these events enhanced the appeal of the group as a patriotic vehicle for ordinary Americans to exercise their political views.[27]

This second phase of the Ku Klux Klan was much broader in its appeals to tradition-minded white American Protestants, and the Klan expanded its targets to include such groups as Jews, Catholics, immigrants and occasionally left-leaning labor and political activists. The early twentieth-century reemergence of the Ku Klux Klan also demonstrated an ability to adapt to local conditions and to tailor its appeal to local and regional concerns. The clichéd aphorism "politics is local" is especially accurate in helping to understand the appeal of the second phase of the Ku Klux Klan.

Understanding the worldview of members of the second phase of the Ku Klux Klan requires twenty-first century readers to set aside present-day moral beliefs and delve into what was "normal" by the standards of the 1920s, at least what was in the realm of "normal" for white Protestants of Anglo-Saxon heritage. The Klan tapped into existing prejudices and beliefs to promote ideologies based on the following general notions:

That there existed a racial hierarchy in which whites of Anglo-Saxon heritage were at the top level.

That "lesser" races needed to be controlled, developed and supervised by whites.

That there existed a conspiracy by Roman Catholics to reinstate the Pope as the supreme power on Earth.

That Jews dominated important industries such as banking and entertainment and that these powerful Jews sought to debase otherwise morally impeccable whites.

That the United States of the 1920s was in a state of moral, political and social crisis, as evidenced by increases in criminal activity.

That there were imminent—though vaguely defined—threats to the future of the American political system.

Some scholars attempt to minimize the importance of white supremacist ideology in Klan recruiting efforts during the 1920s. However, Klan recruitment materials do not attempt to hide the fact that the Klan promoted white supremacy. *America for Americans* was a recruiting pamphlet widely distributed in Wood County in the mid-1920s. The pamphlet declared that "the distinction between the races" was "decreed by the Creator" and that prospective Klan members were required to promise to "be true in the maintenance of White Supremacy."[28]

The second phase of the Klan differed from its earlier incarnation in other ways. In addition to nativist political sentiments, the new Klan also emphasized its role as an arbiter of public morality. Among the most important of the moral issues exploited by the Ku Klux Klan was that of Prohibition, and many Klan

Cover of "America for Americans" pamphlet. *Author's collection.*

chapters attempted to gain legitimacy through efforts—legal as well as illegal—to help law enforcement officials curb the underground trade in alcoholic beverages.

In addition, this regenerated version of the Klan also contained a fraternal component: the second Ku Klux Klan was a secret society with a complex organizational structure, intricate symbolism and clandestine rituals. New inductees to the Ku Klux Klan may have been as enticed by the financial, social and political benefits of joining an organization with millions of members as they might have been by the group's radical ideology. This was a time before safety nets such as Social Security and unemployment compensation, and many American men joined fraternal organizations to protect their families in case of severe financial need.

One of the principal areas of focus for the second Ku Klux Klan was the use of public schools as expressions of the organization's political will. In part, this was an effort to promote what Klan leaders viewed as vital American values (i.e., white Protestant morality), but this was also a means of undermining the Catholic parochial school systems.

A 1924 editorial in the *Wood County Republican* highlights another aspect of the Klan's support of public schools. Citing a study that suggested that there were at least four million illiterate Americans at the time—and "many other semi-educated people who should be placed in the same class"—the author argued that "these ignorant citizens are numerically strong enough to control almost any national election." The problem of illiteracy, intoned the writer, was a "menace to the welfare of America."[29]

The Ku Klux Klan of the 1920s saw public schools as reinforcing the ideals of its "100 Percent Americanism" ideology, and in Ohio, this was especially reflected in the group's support of the 1925 Buchanan-Clark Bible Reading Bill. This law, passed by the Ohio legislature but ultimately vetoed by Governor Vic Donahey, required public school teachers in the state to read Bible verses to their students each day while also requiring older students to commit to memory the Ten Commandments. Donahey, commenting on his decision, argued that the Bible Reading Bill "opposes the principles of civil and religious liberty."[30]

Many residents in Wood County strongly supported the Bible reading legislation. An editorial in the *Wood County Republican* called for readers to "continue their fight for the sort of education that does not leave Christ out of the life of the person educated." Moreover, argued the editorial writer, with a sufficient number of public schools "in which the Bible is read and studied, it is likely that the crime problem in America will solve itself."[31]

?????????????????????????

SHOULD

The Holy Bible

BE HIDDEN FROM

THE YOUTH OF

AMERICA

?

**TWO MILLION COPIES
FIRST DISTRIBUTION**

?????????????????????????

Cover of *Should the Holy Bible Be Hidden from the Youth of America? Author's collection.*

A Ku Klux Klan pamphlet widely distributed in Wood County during the Bible bill debate argued that "the Holy Bible advances civilization." In addition, observed the author of the pamphlet, "future Presidents as well as public servants in their tender age are now in public schools." Opponents of the Bible bill, according to the pamphlet author, were "intolerant," "un-American" and possibly "Communists."[32]

Three other bills were introduced between the years 1923 and 1925 by Ohio legislators who were either Klansmen or Klan-supported. These included efforts to force students in parochial schools to attend public schools (an obvious attack on Catholics), to ban Catholics from teaching in public schools and to make it a criminal offense for ministers to marry a white person and a nonwhite person. While each of these bills failed to pass the legislature, they served as evidence of the growing power of the Ohio Ku Klux Klan to influence the political sphere.

In general, the Klan in Ohio consistently focused on several key goals with regard to public schools. Klan members fought for the prominent display of the Bible and the American flag, and they simultaneously sought to remove any influences they considered "alien" or "foreign." In particular, textbooks in public schools were scrutinized and subject to replacement based on the supposed "alien" or "un-American" ideologies that Klan members detected in them. A 1924 *Wood County Republican* editorial argued that public schools' having regular Bible reading was an ideal way to "Americanize the

Workers at Wood County grain elevator, 1924. *Center for Archival Collections.*

foreigners and enlighten the people." Moreover, noted the writer of the editorial, the "enemies of true Americanism are doing everything possible to keep the Bible out of public schools."[33]

The second phase of the Ku Klux Klan did not burst onto the American scene without philosophical precursors. Racist ideologies, anti-Semitic views, nativist politics and anti-Catholic biases each possessed lengthy precedents in the history of the United States. The resurgent Klan merely provided a convenient vehicle for white Americans (in particular white, Anglo-Saxon, Protestant males) to express these views.

This is not to suggest that the Ku Klux Klan in its second incarnation was unopposed in its growth or that the Klan was not a controversial organization that made many Americans apprehensive. Klan organizers knew exactly what they were doing, and they crafted an adaptable organization that reflected existing mainstream white American views, no matter how repugnant these beliefs might seem to a twenty-first-century reader. A July 26, 1924 edition of the *Wood County Republican* summarized a speech delivered by a national speaker to a large Klonvocation of around two thousand people on farmland outside the city of Bowling Green:

> *The orator of the occasion was from Virginia…by his fearless dealing with the problems of the present day such as boot-legging, law-breaking,*

immigration, the race crisis, the financial peril, and the like, he won for himself round after round of applause.[34]

Klan recruiters and leaders, in a sense, were preaching to the proverbial choir with their ideological messages. The Klan's white supremacist, nativist, anti-Catholic and law-and-order rhetoric meshed well with existing views held by many white Protestant residents of Wood County in the 1920s.

3

RACISM, NATIVISM AND RELIGIOUS INTOLERANCE IN 1920s WOOD COUNTY

The lead cartoon in the October 2, 1923 edition of the *Daily Sentinel-Tribune* would be universally condemned as racist if a twenty-first-century newspaper were to run it. The four-panel sketch featured a white father and daughter going out to dinner, where they encounter an African American waiter with exaggerated features and an almost ape-like demeanor. The cartoonist, Charles McManus, depicted the waiter as a bumbling fool with an exaggerated dialect who seemed incapable of realizing that he was the target of the insults by the white patrons.

While by twenty-first-century standards such a cartoon would be considered offensive, such "entertainment" was common for the time period. Ohio's Wood County was typical of the United States during the 1920s in its embracing of racist, nativist, anti-Catholic and anti-Semitic ideologies.

A 1924 cartoon depicting an African American waiter in a demeaning fashion. *From the Daily Sentinel-Tribune.*

Views that today would generally be considered by most Americans as abhorrent were widely held by white Protestants during the decade of the 1920s. An examination of local newspapers from the 1920s provides revealing vignettes of the existing ethnic, racial and religious prejudices and stereotypes held my many white (especially white Protestant) Wood County residents of the 1920s.

MINSTREL SHOWS IN WOOD COUNTY

Minstrel shows were a relatively frequent occurrence in Wood County in the years leading up to the emergence of the Ku Klux Klan as a political and cultural force in Wood County. Civic, religious and fraternal organizations were the groups most likely to produce a minstrel show, and these were often used as fundraisers for community causes.

These entertainment productions typically featured white performers donning blackface and acting out comedy and musical numbers with characters that portrayed African Americans as dimwitted buffoons or as morally bankrupt individuals deserving of mockery. Some of the minstrel shows also included stereotyped characters portraying Jews, foreigners or disabled persons.

Minstrel shows in the early decades of the twentieth century also served as historical barometers of mainstream white attitudes toward African Americans. Not only were the negative stereotypes and generalizations tolerated, but they were also often well-attended civic events sponsored by social and political elites.

Of particular interest in examining the minstrel shows in Wood County in the 1920s is the presence of a number of prominent civic, business and educational leaders in these productions. Far from being isolated or extremist events, the minstrel shows in Wood County were mainstream extravaganzas that were well attended and that carried a semi-official stamp of approval by local elites.

In advance publicity for the January 20, 1920 minstrel show produced by the Perrysburg Civic Association, the promoters enthused that it "will probably be one of the best home talent entertainments ever given in the Perrysburg Town Hall."[35] Perhaps in a sign that not all Wood County residents supported the inherent racism in minstrel shows, the promoters assured readers that "the entertainment will be excellent in every way and that there will be no cause for regret on the part of anyone attending."[36]

Racism, Nativism and Religious Intolerance in
1920s Wood County

The musical direction of this particular minstrel show was provided by Dr. Dwight Canfield, a local physician who served in a wide variety of civic roles, including his work as a member of the Ohio State Board of Health. The promoters described Dr. Canfield as a director "whose ability in this line is recognized as being of the highest order."[37] It is perhaps not surprising that Dr. Canfield would later be recorded as a charter member of the Wood County Ku Klux Klan.

The director of the blackface extravaganza was John A. Nietz, whose experience in minstrel shows the promoters described as "very favorably known."[38] Mr. Nietz was better known to Perrysburg residents of the time as the superintendent of the Perrysburg public school system, and the family name is still attached to a small airfield north of Bowling Green.

Ticket sales for the 1920 minstrel show were handled by the Perrysburg Women's Community League. Prospective minstrel attendees could also purchase tickets at Champney's Drug Store or at the town hall. Adult tickets for the minstrel show were priced at fifty cents, while children could see the blackface performers for just thirty-five cents. Proceeds from the event went to the Civic Association, and the promoters surmised that this made the event "worthy of the support of every man, woman, and child in the town and county."[39]

The promoters of the minstrel show claimed that it would appeal to people who "love the old plantation songs of long ago" and those who enjoyed "an old-fashioned negro hoe-down."[40] The show also featured a "colored parson" who would be delivering a "most forceful sermon."[41]

The minstrel show, which took place on January 20 and 21, was the "hit of the season,"[42] according to the *Perrysburg Journal*. The newspaper reported that the "Old Time Minstrel Show" played to packed houses each night, and the reviewer of the minstrel show raved about the performances of "many of our prominent businessmen disguised as negroes."[43] The participants in the show were "well lamp-blacked" in their efforts to lampoon African Americans, and one of the highlights of the event was a "Nigger Crap Game"[44] featuring oversized dice and dimwitted characters.

Among the crowd favorites of the musical numbers, described by the *Perrysburg Journal*'s reviewer as "old time darky songs,"[45] were such songs as "Massa's in de Cold, Cold Ground," "Carry Me Back to Old Virginia" and "Old Black Joe." The reviewer proclaimed that the performance "had anything beat this side of New York."[46]

Readers will perhaps not be surprised to learn that John A. Nietz would become a member of the Wood County Ku Klux Klan a few years after his successes in directing the Perrysburg minstrel show.

Later in the year, the members of the Perrysburg Fire Department put on their annual Fireman's Carnival. Despite the fact that several carnival rides did not appear as promised, the *Perrysburg Journal* noted that the carnival "brought a great deal of joy to the kiddies." Among the entertainment highlights of the carnival was a game called the "African Dodger," where a person with a curly wig and blackface attempted to avoid objects thrown at him by carnival-goers, and the refreshments included "nigger babies," which were chocolate confections molded in the shape of small infant humans.[47]

The North Baltimore chapter of the Elks staged a minstrel show in March 1923. This became a production described by the *North Baltimore Times* as "one of the biggest musical hits ever to reach the town."[48] It is not surprising that a number of individuals who would later show up in the Wood County Klan membership lists participated in the minstrel show.

The North Baltimore minstrel show appears to have been somewhat more varied in its racial and ethnic caricatures than the Perrysburg minstrels. This production included an anti-Semitic number entitled the "Yiddish National Anthem," while also containing a "little Irish sketch" that lampooned Irish Catholics. The highlight of the show, however, was a sketch featuring a "reproduction of a colored church" in which a blackface preacher's use of the nursery rhyme "Old Mother Hubbard" for a sermon "convulsed the audience."[49]

The American Legion in the village of Prairie Depot staged a 1924 minstrel show that the *Prairie Depot Observer* reported as being titled the "Darktown Strutters Ball." The event featured "citizens of the community

---

Darktown Strutters Ball

At the Legion Hall Friday night will assemble the citizens of the community dressed in old clothes and black faces. Every lady will is expected to bring one

A headline advertising the "Darktown Strutters Ball." *From the* Prairie Depot Observer.

dressed in old clothes and black faces." Attendees, after donning blackface and seedy clothing, could expect "dancing, games, a pie sale, and a general good time" as they traveled back in time to "Darktown."[50]

Some minstrel shows were performed by students of local public schools. Students from Bloomdale Public Schools participated in a minstrel production titled "Hoop-La" in November 1924. The *Bloomfield Derrick* assured readers that "Hoop-La" was the "funniest of minstrels" and reminded readers that "not every community of this size gets the opportunity for such a High Class show." The minstrel show was produced by John B. Rodgers Producing Company of Fostoria, a director "known throughout the United States" for his work.[51]

RACIST HUMOR

Racist jokes and caricatures were a common occurrence in Wood County newspapers during the 1920s. While disturbing and offensive to most twenty-first-century readers, racist commentary serves to illustrate the widely held underlying ideologies of many residents of the county.

The *Perrysburg Journal* printed the following racist joke in the November 11, 1920 issue of the newspaper; consider here the exaggerated dialect and use of negative stereotypes about African Americans:

> *The other day a negro went into the drug store and said: "Ah wants one of dem plastahs yo' all stick on yo' back."*
> *"I understand," said the clerk. "You mean porous plaster."*
> *"No, sah! Ah don' want none of yo' poorest plastahs. Ah want de bes' yo' all got."* [52]

The *North Baltimore Times* occasionally ran multiple racist jokes in the same issue on a given week, presumably to fill up space on a slow news cycle. The *Times* ran the following demeaning joke in its February 2, 1923 edition; note the use of stereotyped names reminiscent of the slavery era:

> *WHY HE WOULDN'T COME UP*
> *Sambo and Pompey went house robbing, and Pompey wrapped around his body beneath his waistcoat and jacket half a dozen yards of lead piping. In trying to board a Mississippi steamer which was just leaving the dock, he jumped, missed, and fell into the river.*

"Get a boat hook, some of you!" yelled the captain of the steamer. "A man's overboard. He's bound to come up three times."
Up dashed Sambo. "Capen, I bet yer a tenner he doan come up once!"[53]

The racism in the next attempt at humor, also printed in the *North Baltimore Times*, is a bit less overt. Yet some of the same stereotypes about African Americans are present; the piece depicts the black child as uneducated, unsophisticated and prone to being a coward:

AT LEAST HE COULD DO THAT
Little Colored Boy Not Altogether Helpless in the Position of Employer's Protector

An Atlanta woman who had met with financial reverses moved to the country in order to economize. To assist her in odd jobs about the house she engaged a little colored boy named Joe. Now Joe was so pleased with his job that he was anxious to, become a permanent member of the little household.
"Mis' Helen," he began one day, "don't yo' all ever git skeered in dis big house jus' by yo'se'f?"
"Why, yes, Joe," the lady admitted. "It is lonely at times. I have thought, of having someone about when my husband has to be away."
"Well," Joe ventured again, "I jus' thought maybe you'd like to know dat I's a candidate fo' de position of protector in case you decide to employ somebody."
"Why, Joe," said the woman laughing, "what would you do to help me if robbers happened to break in some dark night?"
Joe studied over this for a moment and had an idea.
"Well, Mis' Helen," he said proudly, "dere's one thing I could do in case yo' was visited by unwelcome intruders. I could light the lantern an' show yo'-all which way to run."

Related to the phenomenon of the frequent inclusion of racist jokes in Wood County newspapers was a genre of travel writing that emphasized the backwardness of foreigners, especially Africans. Often these travel narratives were unsigned, as was the case with an October 12, 1923 article in the *North Baltimore Times*.

Entitled "Return to Savage Habits," the information in the article was attributed by the *Times* to "a traveler who has just completed five months' exploration of hitherto unvisited regions of the Tabilia river." The correspondent claimed that French colonial troops in the First World War "returned to their rude huts after having won French war crosses or allied medals for heroism." The unnamed correspondent then launched into a tirade about the backwardness of the former French colonial African troops he allegedly encountered:

> *Instead of adhering to their liking for European clothing and manners, they now parade through the underbrush, girt only in loin clothes* [sic]*, hunting with spears and arrows instead of rifles. Their war decorations are worn on grass chains round their necks, or sometimes pinned in their bushy hair.*[54]

Setting aside the issue that the unnamed narrator referenced a river not found on any contemporary maps, the dubious information contained in the travelogue nonetheless would have resonated with readers, especially newspaper readers in small midwestern towns. Even if the travel narrative was invented in its entirety by the *Times* editor—a distinct possibility, given its lack of verifiable details—readers of the *North Baltimore Times* would not have read anything that conflicted with their views of Africans as backward, uncivilized brutes who needed supervision by whites if they were ever to rise above their lowly rung on the ladder of human civilization.

RACIAL TENSIONS IN 1920s WOOD COUNTY

Racial conflict became significantly more pronounced in Ohio during the decade of the 1920s. In part this was due to the larger number of African Americans in the state as a result of the so-called Great Migration from the South that ramped up during the First World War. Several million African Americans left southern states for cities in the North, Midwest and West in search of better employment opportunities.

Newspapers in Wood County from the 1920s frequently exploited race when it made for sensational headlines. Inevitably any news story involving an African American would identify the individual in terms of race, using words such as "colored," "Negro" or "darkey" to describe the person. This was typically the case even if the news item did not involve a readily apparent reason for the use of specific racial identification (such as the search for a criminal suspect).

An incident involving a group of drifters in a rail yard in Rossford would normally have been buried in a crime or court log section of a newspaper,

BAD NEGROES AT ROSSFORD

Three negroes drifted into the B. & O. railway yards at Rossford Sunday and their actions aroused the

A racially charged 1923 headline. *From the* Wood County Republican.

if it even made the newspaper at all. However, when the incident involved three African American men and one pocketknife, it became front-page news for the *Wood County Republican* in 1923. The headline from the paper was surely geared to heighten the interest of readers for whom concerns about crime and race were important.

The newspaper account noted that after one of the railroad officers was injured in an initial scuffle with the suspect, the other officers "closed in on the darkey with the butts of their guns and gave him a telling reprim." The reporter from the *Wood County Republican* added—with an almost palpable expression of smug satisfaction—that "when they got through with him the prisoner was badly disfigured."

Newspapers in the county frequently hyped news stories involving African Americans that would otherwise be insignificant items if white individuals were involved. One such example was the conviction of an African American man named Evans Parker, convicted of firing a pistol at (but not injuring) another person. The *Wood County Democrat* noted that Parker was in a "cheerful mood" as he awaited transportation to the Ohio State Penitentiary. Parker supposedly told the *Democrat* reporter the following about why his mood was chipper; note the overly caricatured dialogue: "I's a gentleman dat am always lookin' fo a brighter day. I's been goin' to school fo de pass few weeks an' am now goin' to take a course at de state institution, de O.S.P."[55]

White prisoners in an otherwise mundane news item would be unlikely to be interviewed, and details such as vocal inflection or dialect would not be noted even if a white prisoner had been interviewed. The highly detailed focus on an interview subject's dialect merely reinforces perceived differences between the interviewer and the interviewee. This type of reporting also tends to reinforce existing racial stereotypes.

At times, newspapers in Wood County expressed views on race that were extreme even for the time period. A particularly chilling editorial in the *Perrysburg Journal* from February 16, 1922, suggested that the end of slavery was not necessarily a positive outcome for African Americans. The author dutifully reported—based on learned conversations with a southern friend—that "there used to be eighteen or nineteen little pickaninnies running around," whereas now "there are now only eight or nine or ten." The author opined further on the subject:

> *Nearly all the old slavery mothers have died, however, and the new ones have been left to their natural instincts, without any control by the white race. A vast proportion of the* [African American children] *born into the world die before they are of five years of age. Among the negroes the death rate of children under five has increased fearfully in contrast with what it was in slavery times.*[56]

The author summarized that white control of African Americans was the only acceptable "solution," since it was apparent to the author that "negro women are very poor mothers—careless and unintelligent."[57] African Americans, the author claimed, were helpless against the dangers of "whiskey, cocaine, and disease," and only a return to some unspecified form of white control could save them.

Local police forces possessed much greater freedom in their ability to enforce unofficial segregation standards. The January 5, 1923 edition of the *Wood County Democrat* described an incident in which Wood County sheriff Ervin T. Reitzel responded to complaints from Liberty Township residents about an African American man named William Carter who was acting in a "suspicious" manner.

After investigating and finding no evidence of wrongdoing by the fifty-eight-year-old man, the sheriff nonetheless detained the Toledo resident. The paper assured its readers that Parker would be "sent to Toledo by local officials." In perhaps a backhanded attempt at journalistic balance, the paper noted that Carter insisted that he "had no evil intentions,"[58] though of course the inclusion of a loaded phrase such as "evil intentions" by the reporter could also serve as a way to sensationalize an otherwise insignificant incident.

In another example of the use of racially charged headlines, the *Daily Sentinel-Tribune* featured as its top "Court House News" feature the case of Clarence C. Harris. The arrested man, an African American, was accused of failing to pay a room-and-board bill in another city. In the same section in that issue other white defendants were accused of crimes such as assault and robbery. Yet the *Sentinel-Tribune* editors apparently believed that the headline "NEGRO ARRESTED" was of greater interest to readers than stories featuring more serious criminal activity.[59]

In addition, local newspapers consistently placed emphasis on race even in stories that did not involve criminal activity. In a 1923 article about a fire in an apartment in Rossford, the *Daily Sentinel-Tribune* specifically identified all African Americans who were victims of the blaze as "Negro" or "Negros," while the other victims were not identified by any racial or ethnic terms.[60]

Local newspapers also used sensational headlines to highlight racial aspects of articles. In reporting the discovery of a deceased infant near a Perrysburg farm in 1923, the *Daily Sentinel-Tribune* blared the following front-page headline to entice readers: "DEAD NEGRO BABY FOUND IN DITCH."

DEAD NEGRO BABY FOUND IN DITCH

While plowing in a field on his farm four and one-half miles east of Perrysburg where the Glennwood road intersects the Avenue road out of Perrysburg, Henry Limmer, Tuesday noon, found the dead body of

A 1923 headline illustrating selective use of racial identifiers. *From the* Daily Sentinel-Tribune.

The infant was wrapped in a "cloth and a bed comforter," according to the news report. The coroner ruled that the "recently born negro baby" was stillborn. The carefully wrapped corpse suggested that a grieving mother cared for the dead infant after delivery, but a reader would have to dig past the sensationalism to understand the entire sad tale.

Lurid, race-baiting headlines such as these served not only as hooks for newspapers to draw in readers. This journalistic technique also reinforced existing stereotypes and biases, and when the Ku Klux Klan arrived in Wood County, its white supremacist ideology found a ready-made audience.

ANTI-IMMIGRANT AND NATIVIST SENTIMENTS IN 1920s WOOD COUNTY

The state of Ohio, like much of the United States in the 1920s, was an area in which strong nativist and anti-foreigner sentiments had taken hold during and after the First World War. In particular, anti-German hysteria was prominent during this time period due to the role of German-speaking nations as American enemies during the war. These tensions were also heightened due to fears of a hidden fifth column of German Americans in the United States who would undermine the war effort.

In response to continued fears of foreign subversion, the Ohio legislature passed the so-called Ake law in 1919. This act, named after its author, H. Ross Ake, banned the teaching of the German language in all classrooms (both public as well as private) below the eighth-grade level, and this was a law that helped fan the proverbial flames of anti-immigrant attitudes that raged in the country. While the law only applied to classrooms under the eighth-grade level, the pressure to ban the teaching of the German language caused some colleges and high schools to eliminate German courses, including all of the public high schools in Cincinnati.[61] The law was later declared unconstitutional by the U.S. Supreme Court.

The ending of the First World War, interestingly, did not cause much of a change in these strong nativist beliefs. The emergence of anti-Communist hysteria in the United States immediately after the war simply meant that the fear of enemy agents could conveniently be replaced with the fear of the arrival on American shores of waves of radicalized immigrants hellbent on spreading revolution.

The first years of the 1920s in Ohio saw widespread continuation of anti-immigrant sentiments, and Italian, Slavic and Asian immigrants seemed to be the principal sources of concern for Americans with nativist beliefs. Local newspapers from the early 1920s contained frequent denunciations of "undesirable" immigrants.

An editorial printed in 1924 in the *Wood County Republican* argued that "Americans should regard with alarm the fact that nearly one half of the population of the United States is composed of Poles, Russians, Greeks, Italians, Negroes, and European Asiatics." Should these "undesirable" immigrants one day combine their votes, intoned the writer, "they could gain control of the American government."[62]

Fear of immigrant "contamination" was a vital part of the mix of ideologies and biases that the reborn Ku Klux Klan tapped into during the 1920s in Wood County. The surge of anti-immigrant and nativist ideologies was in part tied to fears of communist conspiracies in the years after the 1917 Bolshevik Revolution in Russia. Many native-born Americans associated communism with recent immigrants, especially immigrants from Eastern and southern Europe. The November 25, 1920 *Perrysburg Journal*, for example, reported that Vladimir Lenin planned to send "25,000 spies, 'missionaries,' and agents to the United States to pervert this country to Bolshevism."[63]

Some of the concerns many Americans held regarding immigrants were economic in nature. The *Perrysburg Journal* claimed on January 8, 1920, that "over 100,000 immigrants are on the high seas bound for the United States."[64] The paper reported that 8,500 immigrants passed through Ellis Island in the previous two days and that 50,000 immigrants had entered the United States in the month of December 1919. The news account added the following ominous editorial comment: "If this influx continues there can be no doubt but that wages will tumble before too long."[65]

The *North Baltimore Times* published an editorial on September 21, 1923, that echoed these anti-immigrant sentiments. The editorial writer argued that "the influx of aliens into this country constitutes a lively menace to the peace and prosperity of the United States." The ideal plan for immigration, claimed the editorial, was for "complete cessation" of all immigration into the country. Anyone who opposed immigration restrictions must have a "keen interest in pauper labor," noted the writer, as most immigrants were "practically penniless persons who soon become public charges."[66]

Tirades about immigrants in local papers in Northwest Ohio took a variety of forms. In the June 30, 1921 edition of the *Perrysburg Journal*, a headline belted out that "Koreans Are Very Lazy."[67] The author of the article noted that "it is hardly an exaggeration to say that the Koreans are the laziest people on earth," as members of this ethnic group "lie about the streets smoking their gigantic pipes"[68] the entire day.

Many white Americans in the 1920s considered foreign-born immigrants—especially immigrants from Eastern and southern Europe—to possess lower intellectual abilities than native-born Americans. One writer for the *Perrysburg Journal* blamed persistence of the economic downturn of 1920 and 1921 on the savings habits of immigrants:

> *Business conditions…will show a decided trend for the better on the introduction of this capital which has been hidden away. Foreigners in many localities, not having an intelligent understanding of the safety of recognized financial institutions in their own localities, have been hiding their savings away. These persons must be taught how to make their money work in putting it in sane and safe places. They must be taught to distinguish between the glittering stock certificate with its high interest rates and the savings institution with its fair rate of interest and 100 percent safety factor.*[69]

Americans who held nativist and anti-immigrant beliefs often viewed immigrants as potential sources of moral decay for the United States. In particular, immigrants were frequently depicted as intemperate and prone to drunkenness, traits that would naturally have been seen as threats to the sober morality hypothetically protected by Prohibition.

An August 1921 issue of the *Perrysburg Journal* perpetuated this supposed link between immigrants and alcohol use. The caption accompanying a wire-feed photograph depicted a woman drinking from a cask of wine and suggested that immigrants—in this case an "old Italian woman"—guzzle every last drop of alcohol before their ships reach shore in the United States.

The connection between immigrants and violations of Prohibition laws was frequently made by organizers of the Ku Klux Klan in many parts of the country. This immigration-alcohol theme was the focus of an editorial in the *Wood County Republican* entitled "Deport the Bad Foreigner":

> *Our prohibition laws especially are violated by foreigners. The records of one Justice of the Peace in Lucas County [Ohio] for the year 1922 shows that 70 percent of the 600 violations of the law to be of alien stock, such as Zmiewski, Socolowski, Panoff, Evanoff, Fiatkowski, Katafiasz, Kubacki, Slocinski. This shows who is violating the law in America.*[70]

The Last Drop!

Gurgle! Gurgle! Gurgle! When they are far out at sea immigrants hear about Mr. Volstead and his prohibitory law. And so they drain the last drop from their wine jugs before the boat lands, as did this old Italian woman at Boston.

A 1921 image of an immigrant woman drinking wine. *From the* Perrysburg Journal.

The rhetoric used in the headline by the *Republican* editors suggests an overt attempt to persuade readers of the paper's anti-immigrant stance. Consider the power of the following word choices in the headline "DEPORT THE BAD FOREIGNER" and how a reader in the 1920s would respond to this appeal to political sentiment.

Anti-immigrant sentiments often blended with anti-Catholic biases, and during Prohibition, these views became entangled with beliefs that immigrant Catholics were among the worst violators of Prohibition laws. A news article that devolved into an editorial in the *Wood County Republican* argued that the

THURSDAY, JULY 12th, 1923

DEPORT THE
BAD FOREIGNER

A 1923 front-page editorial illustrating nativist sentiments. *From the* Wood County Republican.

town of Rossford was "building around its sacred precincts a reputation for crime and disregard for the law that will very soon place the city among the most notorious regions of Northwestern Ohio."

Rossford's troubles, according to the writer for the *Republican*, stemmed from its "large percentage of foreign-born residents." These immigrants, according to the article, "have been reared in countries that have but slight regard for moderation in the use of intoxicating beverages."[71]

Fear of larger cities as centers of lawless immigrants was a theme that resonated in Wood County newspapers in the 1920s. An example of this anti-immigrant hysteria can be seen in a 1923 editorial published by the *North Baltimore Times*. Commenting on a recent bombing, the *Times* editor claimed that "Toledo is fast becoming afflicted with foreign nihilists and anarchists who regard every person who has reached a competency an enemy." The editorial demanded that it was "time to put up the bars against the reckless foreign emigration," and the editorial writer claimed that "practically all the labor trouble in this country" could be traced to immigrants.[72] The headline of the article, "ANARCHISTS IN TOLEDO," underscored the fear of immigrant-based criminal activity.

Immigrants were closely associated in the minds of many native-born Americans with criminal activity. An editorial in the August 28, 1924 edition of the *Wood County Republican* argued that "criminals are very largely recruited from the ranks of aliens who arrive here with little or no respect for the laws of the country." The writer claimed that there were over one million "alien criminals," and that the "presence of so many criminals in America is both a moral and economic danger." The writer opined that there could be nothing worse than the degrading influence of one million moral degenerates" who are "free to spread their rotten influence among both young and old."[73]

BELGIAN ARRESTED

W. W. Mountain, Belgian was arrested by the North Baltimore officers Saturday night. The police claim a gallon of WHITE MULE was found on him. He was arranged before the Mayor and fined $150 and costs which he paid.

A 1923 headline selectively highlighting the ethnic origin of a defendant. *From the* Wood County Republican.

Violations of laws related to Prohibition by immigrants often became front-page news when the infraction was committed by an immigrant, even if the person was a naturalized citizen. The March 14, 1923 edition of the *Wood County Republican* trumpeted the case of a man named W.W. Mountain who was caught in North Baltimore with illegal alcohol.

The defendant in question had become an American citizen many years earlier. However, the sensationalism of the "bad foreigner" motif was too tempting for *Wood County Republican* editors to pass up in this example. The "WHITE MULE" reference was a phrase deliberately selected to influence readers, as terms such as "corn liquor" or "illegal alcohol" would not have carried the same connotations of danger as "white mule" would.

Another example of the "bad foreigner" theme being casually applied by a newspaper involved the 1923 arrest of a laundry owner named Charles Sing. The business owner was targeted in raid of several Rossford buildings, and sheriff's deputies discovered two cases of homebrewed beer. Despite the fact that Sing was a U.S. citizen born in California in 1875,[74] the *Wood*

CHINESE GRABBED AT ROSSFORD ON LIQUOR CHARGE

A 1923 headline highlighting the ethnic origins of a defendant. *From the* Daily-Sentinel Tribune.

County Republican repeatedly referred to him as a "Chinaman" in a front-page article, while the cases of numerous white individuals arrested for violators of liquor laws were limited to one-sentence summaries buried in the middle of the paper.[75]

The case of Charles Sing also caught the attention of the *Daily Sentinel-Tribune*. Once again, the arrested man was described as a "Chinaman" in the account, and the terms "Chinese," "China" or "Chinaman" were used throughout the article. Sing, according to the *Daily Sentinel-Tribune*, paid for his bond with "bills of small denomination which he had concealed in his laundry," a curious and somewhat inflammatory detail that suggests an intent to sway public opinion on the part of either the reporter or the police department. However, the ethnicities of the other two defendants arrested in the sweep were not noted in the newspaper account.[76]

Use of the plural "Chinese" implies that more than one person was involved in the raid, perhaps suggesting a criminal gang or network. The term "grabbed" implies some sort of violent struggle in an otherwise mundane arrest. Interestingly, the paper chose to use the word "liquor" in the headline despite the fact that the raid turned up a total of two cases of "homemade brew."[77]

EXISTING ANTI-SEMITIC AND ANTI-CATHOLIC VIEWS IN 1920s WOOD COUNTY

There was nothing especially unique about anti-Semitic views held by residents of Northwest Ohio in the decades between the First and Second World Wars. Anti-Semitic stereotypes and caricatures were widely embraced by many white Americans in the period, and mainstream newspapers in Wood County regularly contained hints of the anti-Semitism that would become a key pillar of the Ku Klux Klan's emergence in the region.

The June 30, 1921 edition of the *Perrysburg Journal* contained an odd (and inaccurate) news story about the inventor of the crown bottle cap, which the paper identified as a man named "Taintor." The inventor's real name was William Painter, and the multimillion-dollar business that he created is today part of Crown Holdings, Inc., a corporation headquartered in Philadelphia.

In the news item, though, the inventor "Taintor" was an impoverished man with an idea for the bottle cap, and it took a "traveling Jew peddler" named "Friedenwaldt" to make the dream become a reality. The Jew, according to the news item, sold "jewelry and nicknacks [*sic*]" in his travels, and the bottle cap became a ubiquitous accessory in the bottling industry only through the machinations of the Friedenwaldt character, a person who in some ways resembles the historical meme of the "wandering Jew."

The November 23, 1923 edition of the *North Baltimore Times* contained the following example of the types of anti-Semitic jokes that frequently appeared in local Wood County newspapers in the 1920s. (A "flivver" is an outdated expression for an automobile of low quality in need of numerous repairs, akin to later terms such as "jalopy" or "beater car"):

> *Two gentlemen of Hebraic extraction, joint owners of a flivver, were hauled into court on the charge of driving with only one headlight. The Hebraic gentlemen pled guilty and were fined $10 and costs.*
>
> *"Vell," said one of the partners, "the easiest vay to settle the matter is for each of us to pay half. Ve both own the car, and ve vas both in it."*
>
> *"No, no!" exclaimed the other. "My side vasn't out! My side vasn't out!"*[78]

The *North Baltimore Times* provided another example of the use of anti-Semitic humor in local newspapers:

Probably a Klansman
"What are rabies and what would you do for them?" read a query in a
recent civil service examination.
"Rabies are Jewish priests and I wouldn't do a darn thing for them,"
was the unexpected reply of one applicant.[79]

Another of the principal components of Klan ideology was the organization's embrace of strong anti-Catholic views. The typical Klansman believed that the Roman Catholic Church secretly conspired to take control of the American government with an ultimate goal of the Pope relocating to Washington, D.C. In particular, Catholic parochial schools were eyed with great suspicion, both in terms of "indoctrinating" students and undermining "100 percent Americanism."

The idea of Catholics as persons with divided loyalties and as part of an un-American fifth column stretches far back in American history. These views were widely held by many Protestants in the late nineteenth and early twentieth centuries, while to a lesser extent, Protestants of a more fundamentalist bent believed that the Catholic Church was the Whore of Babylon described in the Book of Revelation.

Klan organizers made wide use of printed anti-Catholic propaganda to reinforce and strengthen existing anti-Catholicism. An example of this genre was a pamphlet entitled *The Church of Rome in American Politics: Making America Catholic.* The anonymous author contracted with a publishing house in Missouri called the Menace Publishing Company, and the pamphlet's first printing appears to have occurred in 1912. Klan members in Wood County used the pamphlet in their recruiting efforts, and numerous copies have survived.

The pamphlet contains nearly fifty pages of half-truths, outright lies and scurrilous disinformation about the Roman Catholic Church. The author claimed that the Pope had arrived at the conclusion that the future success of the Catholic Church "depends on its conquest of America in the next decade."[80] According to the author, "75 percent of the employees of the government are Catholic," and the country was already under Catholic control "in a political sense."[81]

According to the author of the pamphlet, a "good Catholic cannot possibly be a Good Citizen of this nation at one and the same time"[82] due to supposed conflicting loyalties to the state and the church. The Catholic Church, in the eyes of the author, was the "most dangerous menace to this country, this government, our free institutions, and all the principles at the foundation of Popular Free Government."[83]

Another theme discussed in the anti-Catholic pamphlet that meshed with the policy goals of the Ku Klux Klan was federal funding for public education. The cover of the pamphlet contained a cartoon that succinctly summarized Klan views on the importance of public education. The drawing depicted a public school building with the ominous declaration "ANTIDOTE TO PAPAL POISON."

Anti-Catholic sentiments frequently worked their way into a number of Wood County newspapers in the 1920s. A 1924 editorial in the *Wood County Republican* that drew heavily from Klan literature argued that "Catholicism in America is nothing short of a gigantic political machine directed by a foreign ruler, dominated by foreign ideals, and antagonistic to American principles and policies." Catholics, according to the editorial writer, were vastly outnumbered by Protestants in the United States. In addition, most Catholics were best seen as "foreigners who have not and may never become American citizens."[84]

The initial organizers and recruiters fielded by the Ku Klux Klan in Wood County in late 1922 arrived in an area in which racist, nativist, and intolerant views were already present. This made the work of attracting Wood County residents to the Klan that much easier.

4

THE GROWTH OF THE KU KLUX KLAN IN WOOD COUNTY

Frank W. Rogers found himself in an especially difficult situation on February 18, 1924. The veteran Bowling Green police officer walked out of the city safety director's office that day with news that he was suspended for "malfeasance and misfeasance as an officer."[85] He might also have faced criminal charges for actions he took while working as a police officer.

Rogers had been enthusiastic in carrying out his duties, especially his work in upholding Prohibition laws. Local newspaper accounts from the 1920s attest to the frequent arrests made by Rogers of bootleggers, scofflaws and still operators. In the winter of 1924–25, Rogers even used his own Essex automobile on the job, since the city of Bowling Green did not have a police cruiser and he could not use the department's motorcycle "on account of severe weather conditions."[86]

As Rogers crossed the interurban tracks in downtown Bowling Green after receiving news of his suspension, he would have been weighing his options.

By his own admission, Rogers decided that the uncompensated wear and tear on his vehicle needed to be addressed. Rogers went into the impound lot and removed from a "confiscated booze car" a set of tires and a pair of "Gabriel snubbers" (precursors to the shock absorbers today found on motor vehicles). He then installed the tires and suspension system on his own vehicle.

Unfortunately for Rogers, his actions were observed by city employees, and city safety director solicited affidavits from the witnesses regarding the theft of confiscated property. As a result, Rogers faced the possibility not only of losing his job but also the outside possibility of theft charges. The

Interurban car in Bowling Green. *Center for Archival Collections.*

sworn testimony of the witnesses seemed to be damning pieces of evidence against him.

Rogers did have one very important factor weighing in his favor that winter: he was a charter member of the Wood County Ku Klux Klan, and he had powerful fraternal friends in high places.

The day after his suspension, the pro-Klan *Wood County Republican* ran an incendiary front-page article entitled "Charity Suffereth Long and Is Kind," a veiled reference to a biblical verse in 1 Corinthians, chapter 13. The writer of the article claimed that "Officer Rogers has been made the scapegoat," and the author threatened that "when all is over some startling facts may be revealed." The article claimed that "confiscated cars have been used by city officials...for public and private use," and the writer closed by urging "every citizen that knows of wrongs being practiced to expose them that our city may be purged of any filth that may exist."[87]

Yet despite his admission of wrongdoing and the sworn depositions of several witnesses regarding the theft, Rogers was reinstated on the police force a few weeks later. No explanation for the about-face was provided by safety director Earl K. Solether, and in the reinstatement letter Solether benevolently suggested that the removal of tires and snubbers by Rogers was a "mistake" and that the officer took the items "with the best of intentions."[88]

No record exists of behind-the-scenes advocacy performed on behalf of Frank Rogers, but the influence of many important city and county officials who happened to be Klan members could not have hurt the cause of the suspended officer. At the time of the incident, for example, the county prosecutor and at least two Bowling Green city council members were Kluxers, and the suspension of fellow Klan member Rogers could not have been overlooked. In the mid-1920s, the Klan wielded impressive political power in Wood County, and it would be naïve to think that a non-Klansman like Solether would not have at least paused to consider the possible repercussions of firing or prosecuting a Klansman with so many friends in high places.

ORIGINS OF THE KLAN IN OHIO

It is difficult to say with a high degree of precision the exact date in which the Ku Klux Klan began its activities in Ohio. The earliest date in which Klan organizers have been documented to be actively recruiting new members in the state of Ohio was in the fall of 1920, prior to the presidential election that year.[89]

In a September 30, 1921 edition of the *Cleveland Plain Dealer*, a news item discussed a four-hour interview that the Cleveland police chief conducted with the Grand Goblin of the Great Lakes region, a man named Charles W. Love. While Love's claims of fifteen thousand Klan members in Ohio in 1921 may be boastful or overstated,[90] it is certain that the year of 1921 marked a noticeable uptick in Klan activity in the Buckeye State.

The date of September 30 is also significant in that Cuyahoga County prosecutor Edward Stanton refused to send a case against the Ohio Ku Klux Klan to a grand jury. Stanton noted that "no evidence has been offered by anyone unsympathetic to the Klan which would warrant taking the matter to the grand jury." While hardly a ringing endorsement of the Klan, Stanton's actions nonetheless undoubtedly brought a sigh of relief to Ohio's Klansmen: if the legal system in one of the state's largest cities—one with significant African American, immigrant and Catholic populations—refused to act, surely the Klan would find an easier time operating in rural and small town settings in Ohio.

Klan ideology and recruiting strategies proved extremely successful in Ohio, and Klan chapters rapidly formed throughout the state. By the end of 1923, there were likely more than 300,000 Klan members in the Buckeye State, which proved to be a numerical and financial windfall for the national Klan organization. The *Columbus Dispatch* in 1925 reported that there were at least 108 active Klaverns in the state of Ohio at that time, with 14 Klaverns in Hamilton County alone.[91]

A significant number of membership records of the Wood County Ku Klux Klan have survived and are now stored at the Center for Archival Collections at Bowling Green State University. The earliest records date back to the beginning of the year 1924, but it is clear that the group was quite active in 1923 and likely as early as the last few months of 1922.

A partial accounting journal dating from January 1, 1924, begins at the number 501, suggesting that there may have been as many as 500 additional entries of the payment of dues prior to January 1924.[92] In the years 1924 and 1925, nearly 1,400 individuals paid dues to the Wood County Ku Klux Klan, and in 1924, Kluxers formed a separate chapter of the Klan in Perrysburg. Approximately 150 of the Wood County Klan members migrated to the new Perrysburg Klavern that year.

The *Wood County Republican* newspaper noted in its March 15, 1923 edition that a branch of the Ku Klux Klan was started "about a month ago," making southern Wood County a site of significant Klan activity as early as February 1923.[93] In the August 14, 1923 edition of the *Wood County Republican*, the paper's reporter indicated that a Klan source informed him that the "Wood County Klan will charter in later September [1923] when the remaining counties of the state receive their charters."[94]

The granting of a charter to the Wood County Klan represented an important milestone for the group. Not only was this a moment of pride for the group to become a stand-alone Klan chapter, but also portions of the initiation and dues charged to members could stay in the local unit for expenditures as opposed to remitting all of these funds to the Realm offices.

The Klan operated quite openly in Wood County during its years as a political and cultural force in the region. Unlike chapters in the other parts of the country—and certainly different from later incarnations of the Klan— the organization found little need to keep its activities especially secretive. As late as 1930, the group continued to operate out of a storefront on South Main Street in downtown Bowling Green.

WHO WERE THE MEMBERS OF THE WOOD COUNTY KLAN?

The 1920 census recorded 44,892 residents in Wood County, and at least 1,390 of those residents at one point belonged to the Ku Klux Klan. The total number of Wood County residents who at one point were members of the Klan was thus a little over 3 percent of the total population. Women and children were not permitted to join the Klan, and in the 1920 census, children under eighteen represented about 37 percent of the total population.[95] Factoring out women, children, Catholics, persons of color and immigrants reduces the pool of native-born white male adult Protestants to about 9,600 persons. Thus, the percentage of eligible Wood County residents who joined the Klan was approximately 15 percent of the population.

Several communities appear to have had much higher rates of Klan membership than the norm. Part of the discrepancy is the reliance on Klan membership records to identify a particular community, as these do not necessarily line up with specific census designations. Klan membership records likely represent how a Kluxer self-identified in terms of residence at the time of applying to join the Klan, though it is possible that the Klan official recording residence information may have categorized individuals into particular municipal categories.

In addition, some villages appear to have over-representation due to Klan members from surrounding townships identifying themselves with a particular village. This seems to be the case with the high rates of Klan membership in the villages of Portage (18.48 percent) and Rudolph (13.04 percent).

Several of the towns with the highest rates of Klan membership—such as Portage, Cygnet, Rudolph and North Baltimore—were located on the historical Dixie Highway. This road was a major conduit of north–south traffic and was one of the principal routes by which African Americans traveled north during the First Great Migration. It is possible that the greater visibility of African Americans on this road may have heightened fears or perceived danger by white residents in communities such as Portage.

An analysis of Wood County Ku Klux Klan membership records reveals interesting general information about the typical Kluxer. The average Klan member in Wood County spent 3.35 years in the group, and the average Klan member was 38.58 years of age at the time of joining the Klan. Klan members ranged in age from 18 to 76 at the time they joined the Wood County Klan.

A total of 102 members of the Wood County Klan attained the prestigious status of K-Trio, the third level of membership in Klan hierarchy. Most

TABLE 3
Wood County Klan Membership by Municipality

MUNICIPALITY	TOTAL	TOTAL KLAN	KLAN AS PERCENTAGE OF TOTAL RESIDENTS
Portage	303	56	18.48
Rudolph	652	85	13.04
Prairie Depot	578	59	10.21
Weston	844	72	8.53
Cygnet	521	41	7.87
Bowling Green	5,788	426	7.36
Custar	316	23	7.28
Bairdstown	158	10	6.33
Milton Center	194	12	6.19
Haskins	427	25	5.85
North Baltimore	2,438	133	5.46
Walbridge	532	28	5.26
Tontogany	603	27	4.48
Luckey	249	10	4.02
Perrysburg	2,429	97	3.99
Bloomdale	509	19	3.73
Millbury	226	8	3.54
Grand Rapids	517	17	3.29
Hoytville	367	8	2.18
Pemberville	938	17	1.81
Jerry City	266	4	1.50
Ross Township	4,184	62	1.48
Bradner	785	10	1.27
Risingsun	477	6	1.26

K-Trio members hit this milestone in their fourth year with the Klan, with 1928 being the year in which the most K-Trio designations were bestowed on members.

In numerical terms, the occupations that composed the largest segment of Klan membership in Wood County were farmers and agricultural laborers. These individuals represented at least 284 Klansmen in the mid-1920s, or approximately 20.4 percent of all Wood County Klan members. These individuals likely found the economic and nativist arguments of the Klan most appealing, given the declines in farm values and commodity prices plus

Ragamuffin Parade in Portage, Ohio. *Center for Archival Collections.*

Unidentified oil workers near Cygnet, Ohio, 1920. *Center for Archival Collections.*

Table 4
Occupations of Wood County Ku Klux Klan Members

Occupation	Total Klansmen	Percentage of Total Klansmen
Farmer	242	17.41
Oil worker	146	10.50
Salesman	55	3.96
Railroad worker	54	3.88
Owner (retail business)	46	3.31
Mechanic	44	3.17
Truck driver	43	3.09
Agricultural laborer	42	3.02
Factory worker	41	2.95
Carpenter	40	2.88
Clerk	36	2.59
Machinist	28	2.01
Glass worker	27	1.94
Minister	23	1.65
Teacher/school official	19	1.37
Sheriff deputy/police officer	19	1.37
Manager	18	1.29
Postal worker	15	1.08
Physician/chiropractor	14	1.01
Foreman	13	0.94
Butcher	13	0.94
Painter	12	0.86
Mason/bricklayer	12	0.86
Barber	12	0.86
Electrician	11	0.79
Insurance salesman	9	0.65
Restaurant worker	8	0.58
Quarry worker	8	0.58
Grain elevator worker	8	0.58
Contractor (buildings)	8	0.58
Bank employee	8	0.58
Blacksmith	7	0.50
Welder	6	0.43
Lawyer	6	0.43
Engineer	5	0.36
Autoworker	5	0.36

fears of low-wage immigrants further eroding the incomes of Americans engaged in agricultural occupations. This would have been especially true of farm owners and agricultural landlords.[96]

One group that Wood County Klan recruiters seem to have targeted and achieved significant success in their efforts to grow membership was oil industry workers. Though petroleum output was on the decline by the 1920s in the county, there were still many hundreds of workers involved in the extraction, shipment, and refinement of crude oil in Wood County.

Approximately 146 members of the Wood County Klan worked in various capacities of the county's diminishing oil industry. Census records indicate many workers with jobs such as "roustabout," "driller," "pumper" and "switcher." The presence of oil company foremen and owners in the Klan membership lists suggests that these workers may have been influenced, or even prodded, by company officials to join the Ku Klux Klan.

Sales-related work was another occupational field in which Klan recruiters found many willing prospects. Salesmen, regardless of the strength of their belief in Klan ideology, very likely viewed the Klan as a potentially valuable source of business contacts and clients. Klan recruiters certainly pitched the networking possibilities of joining the group in their presentations to salesmen.

The appeal of the Ku Klux Klan to workers in the railroad and interurban industries is more difficult to assess. The Klan typically exhibited a fair degree of hostility toward labor movements, though, in the national railroad strike of 1922, the Klan did support railroad workers in their efforts to improve wages and working conditions.[97] The large number of railroad and interurban workers in the Wood County Klan might reflect an attempt by Klan recruiters to depict the Klan as an organization friendly to union rail workers.

KLAN RECRUITING TECHNIQUES IN WOOD COUNTY

The Klan utilized a wide variety of tactics in its efforts to recruit Wood County citizens to its ranks. The organization's kleagles proved adept at modifying their messages to appeal to the views held by different segments of the white population.

Klan members passed out introduction cards to prospective members as one of the initial strategies. These cards generally lacked specific details, and instead simply used vague terms such as "patriotic" and "important" to entice targeted citizens to attend a meeting. Often the introduction cards

THE PAUL REVERE CLUB

Invites You to Attend a

Patriotic Mass Meeting

Date_____ Time_____

Place _____

Admit Mr. _____

It Is Very Important That You Present This Card

Issued by _____

"Paul Revere Club" card used by the KKK to recruit new members in Wood County. *Center for Archival Collections.*

Old Glory Club

OPEN AIR MEETING

Place_____

_____

Time_____

Admit Mr._____

Address_____

Recommended by_____

"Old Glory Club" card used by the KKK to recruit new members in Wood County. *Center for Archival Collections.*

carried deceptive or misleading names; in Wood County the names "Paul Revere Club" and "Old Glory Club" seem to have been the names most frequently used by the Klan to conceal recruitment meetings.

The introduction cards served two distinct purposes. The cardholder would be able to attend the given function, making the card the equivalent of an admission ticket. The introduction card also created an implicit sense of value for the recipient, and the event became more exclusive and vital in the eyes of the cardholder.

Detailed information about the recruiting practices of the Ku Klux Klan in Wood County is somewhat limited. The *Wood County Democrat* reported in August 1924 that select county residents had received invitation cards to a Klan function with "the printed name of Karl Dickman, I.T.S.U.B."[98] The coded acronym was a Klan sign-off used in correspondence that meant "In the Sacred Unfailing Bond."

As was the case with other KKK chapters, the Wood County Klan frequently tapped existing organizations to identify and target recruits. Especially useful for recruiting purposes were existing fraternal organizations. Groups such as the Free and Accepted Masons, the Woodsmen, the International Order of Odd Fellows, the American Legion and the Benevolent and Protective Order of Elks provided the Klan with access to people who were already inclined to join a fraternal organization.

In some cases these organizations already contained as members Klan organizers who joined the KKK after they became members of other fraternal groups. In other cases, kleagles and other recruiters joined organizations for the sole purpose of making inroads with potential recruits, occasionally even going so far as to obtain by surreptitious means membership lists of other fraternal groups.

Klan robe order form.
Center for Archival Collections.

The late nineteenth and early twentieth centuries have occasionally been described by scholars as a sort of "golden age" for fraternal organizations in the United States. Not only was membership by Americans in fraternal groups widespread, but also a person who joined one fraternal group was significantly more likely to join additional fraternal organizations. Klan organizers in the 1920s were acutely aware of the role that fraternal groups could play in the growth of the KKK.

Civic and business organizations were additional avenues for the Klan to exploit for potential recruits. Individuals who joined Wood County organizations such as the Commercial Club, the Dry Federation, the Anti-Saloon League and the Wood County Auto Club were already inclined to be concerned about local political and economic issues, and the Klan infiltrated or exploited connections in these organizations to bolster its recruiting efforts.

The Klan's recruitment staff was careful to tailor the group's message to fit the existing beliefs of the region in which it sought to build membership. Certainly one of the messages that resonated quite strongly among potential Klansmen in Wood County was the group's anti-immigrant views.

At a 1923 Klonklave in Bowling Green, an unidentified Klan officer spoke before a massive crowd at the Wood County Fairgrounds. The Klan favored a ban on immigration, he said, because "it will not be long before this 'melting pot' will boil over if all immigration is not stopped." Americans, the Klan speaker claimed, "have not been able to assimilate the immigrants in their body politic."[99]

Once accepted into the group, new Klansmen would be fitted for robes and hoods (the Klan uses the term "helmet" for the headgear). Measurements would be taken at the local Klavern, and the tailoring information would be submitted to the national Klan headquarters.

THE KLAN'S USE OF PROTESTANT MINISTERS IN RECRUITMENT

Perhaps the most important ingredient in the growth of Klan in Wood County was the group's use of Protestant ministers to help with member recruiting, to provide organizational leadership, and to add moral legitimacy to the group. The Wood County Klan records contain the names of at least twenty-three Protestant ministers who became naturalized Klan members, a figure that represents nearly 40 percent of the Protestant clergy in the county at the time.

A national Klan speaker who visited North Baltimore in 1924 acknowledged the importance of Protestant ministers in building the organization. Protestant churches, he observed, could best be described as the "back of this movement." The speaker added that Protestant churches "are so closely related to the Klan that one cannot tell where one leaves off and the other begins."[100] This close association between Klan and Protestant clergy was most certainly the case in the history of the Wood County Ku Klux Klan.

By far the denomination in Wood County with the largest number of ministers as Klan members was the United Brethren Church. The denomination known as Church of the United Brethren in Christ was founded in 1800 by Martin Boehm and Philip William Otterbein, pastors in Pennsylvania with connections to the Mennonite and Wesleyan traditions. The United Brethren Church went through a series of mergers later in the twentieth century and today is part of the United Methodist Church.

A significant reason for the importance of the United Brethren Church in the rise of the Klan in Wood County is simply sheer numbers. The UBC was the largest denomination at the time in terms of numbers of churches, with a UBC congregation in almost every town in the county with a population over five hundred. The UBC's historical connection to ethnic Germans in the region is another reason for its local prominence as a Protestant denomination.

The church also possessed a local leader with impressive organizational, motivational and oratorical ability: the Reverend Rush A. Powell. In addition to his lengthy tenure as minister of the largest UB church in the county, Trinity United Brethren in Bowling Green, Reverend Powell also served as a district superintendent for the UBC. His administrative duties meant that he frequently traveled to regional UB churches, and his network of UB minister contacts certainly benefited the Klan.

It is not certain that Reverend Powell directly used his position as an administrator in the UBC to foster Klan expansion efforts by providing congregation lists to the KKK. More likely the connections between Powell and Klan growth were more associative in nature, with the reverend making introductions between Klan organizers and local UBC ministers or with Reverend Powell simply promoting the group to his subordinate ministers. However, Powell was, by contemporary accounts, a riveting speaker who possessed a remarkable level of charisma, and the Ku Klux Klan in Wood County benefitted greatly from having someone with his abilities within the ranks of the group.

Trinity Church in Risingsun, Ohio. *Center for Archival Collections.*

In addition to the twenty-three known ministers in Wood County who were active Klan members, other Protestant clergy members were certainly sympathetic to the cause even if they never joined the Klan. At least two dozen additional churches without known Klan ministers received Klan "visits" in the form of interruptions to worship services, and most of these "visits" were prearranged affairs in which the minister was at least aware that the group intended to march into the service.

In some cases there was even public notice printed of the upcoming Klan activities in local churches. The January 8, 1925 edition of the *Wood County Republican* contained a front-page news item entitled "Klan Night." The paper reported that it was "strongly rumored that a robed delegation will visit the church on this occasion." The "Klan Night" activities, according to the newspaper account, also included a farewell address by the Reverend Hiram N. Van Voorhis, who was soon to take a new position at another Church of Christ congregation. Reverend Van Voorhis, not surprisingly, was one of the many Wood County ministers who were listed on the membership rolls of the Ku Klux Klan.

Among the Protestant ministers who were quite open regarding their membership in the Ku Klux Klan was the Reverend John W. Wilch, whose congregation was the Bloomdale Methodist Episcopal Church. Reverend Wilch spoke at numerous Klan events, including a "100 Percent American" speech he delivered in 1923 on behalf of the Wood County Klan at an auditorium in Prairie Depot. A "good sized audience" at the facility heard Reverend Wilch deliver a "most excellent address" in which the minister "encouraged the organizing of all who believe in the preservation of the National Constitution." Reverend Wilch, according to the correspondent for the *Prairie Depot Observer*, "spoke highly of the principles of the Klansmen."[101]

WOMEN, CHILDREN AND THE WOOD COUNTY KLAN

As a male-only organization, the Ku Klux Klan barred women from joining the group. However, the organization encouraged the formation of auxiliary Klan units for women and children. The Klan in Wood County supported the creation of such units, and each of these auxiliary Klan organizations was quite active in the mid-1920s.

No official records of the auxiliary Klans of Wood County are known to have survived, and newspaper accounts provide several different names for these units. The most common phrase used to describe women's Klan groups in Wood County was "Ladies of the Wood County Court of the Ku Klux Klan," which appeared in numerous articles in the *Wood County Republican* in 1923 and 1924. "Ladies of the Klan" and "Klan ladies" are two additional terms used several times in mid-1920s newspaper accounts.

The Kreed of the Women of the Ku Klux Klan shares many similarities to the oath taken by male members of the Klan. Women making the pledge agreed that they would be "devoted to the sublime principles of a pure Americanism." The Kreed also required women to "avow the distinction of the races of mankind as decreed by the Creator." Moreover, women who agreed to become auxiliary Klan members had to promise to be "true to the maintenance of White Supremacy and strenuously oppose any compromise thereof."[102]

The women's auxiliary Klan unit received external assistance in its creation. The *Wood County Republican* noted that a "great amount of work has been done by the new lady organizer who comes into Wood County determined to make a real ladies organization in Wood County."[103]

Women of
The Ku Klux Klan

KREED
(Original Creed Revised)

We, the Order of the Women of the Ku Klux Klan, reverentially acknowledge the majesty and supremacy of Almighty God and recognize His goodness and providence through Jesus Christ, our Lord.

Recognizing our relation to the Government of the United States of America, the supremacy of its Constitution, the Union of States thereunder, and the Constitutional Laws thereof, we shall ever be devoted to the sublime principles of a pure Americanism, and valiant in the defence of its ideals and institutions.

We avow the distinction between the races of mankind as decreed by the Creator, and we shall ever be true to the maintenance of White Supremacy and strenuously oppose any compromise thereof.

We appreciate the value of practical, fraternal relationship among people of kindred thought, purpose and ideals and the benefits accruing therefrom; we shall faithfully devote ourselves to the practice of an honorable clannishness that the life of each may be a constant blessing to others.

"Non Silba Sed Anthar."

Imperial Headquarters, Little Rock, Ark.

Form 840—J.F.H.

Women of Ku Klux Klan Kreed. *Center for Archival Collections.*

The September 21, 1923 edition of the *North Baltimore Times* reported that a "large number" of women attended a recruiting event for the women's Klan auxiliary. The event took place at the Hotel Columbia in North Baltimore, and a female lecturer employed by the Klan discussed the merits of joining the organization. It appears that recruiting cards had been circulated prior to the event, as the news account added that "admission was by card."[104]

The women's Klan auxiliaries tended to be involved with charitable and social events related to the Klan's goal. The March 6, 1924 edition of the *Wood County Republican* described a "chicken supper" held by Klan women at the Woodmen Hall in Bowling Green. The event featured a national speaker, and afterward, "music was furnished by an orchestra." The reporter duly noted that a "neat sum was realized from the supper," suggesting that the group intended the event as a fundraiser.[105]

Women of the Wood County Klan appear to have used fundraising events in an effort to provide revenue for charitable work. The April 3, 1924 edition of the *Wood County Republican* reported a donation made to an "elderly couple" in the village of Rudolph. The donation to Phillip Chamberlain and his wife consisted of "several dollars and a large basket of eatables," and the group selected the couple because Chamberlain—a maintenance worker at a church with close Klan ties—had been "seriously ill for some weeks."[106]

The women in the Wood County auxiliary Klan were also involved in planning and managing events that were focused ostensibly toward male Klan members. Newspaper accounts of most Klan events in the 1920s discuss various roles played by Klan women. The October 30, 1924 *Wood County Republican* covered a major Klonklave at the Wood County Fairgrounds that occurred earlier in the week, and the paper noted that "Lady Klan members contributed their share in making the Klonklave a success, both by assisting and being in the line of march."[107]

The Klan targeted children as a way to more closely align families with the group. In addition, children represented the best source of future Klan members, as the "100 Percent American" values espoused by the group could be instilled in children at an early age. To help achieve its goals, the Klan developed children's auxiliary groups such as the Junior Ku Klux Klan.

An advertisement for the Junior Ku Klux Klan appeared in 1924 in the *Wood County Republican*. The Junior Klan, according to the advertisement, would instruct boys and girls in such topics as "reverence toward God," "the value of a clean, moral life," "the purity of our Womanhood," and the importance "to maintain forever White Supremacy."

It is unclear the extent to which the Junior Ku Klux Klan or similar youth-oriented Klan organizations took hold in Wood County. There are passing references to such organizations in organizational records and newspaper accounts, but other than brief mentions, the topic is not well documented in existing sources on the KKK in Wood County.

The *North Baltimore Times* reported on February 29, 1924, that regional Klan chapters purchased athletic sweaters for local high school sports teams. The paper noted that the "Triple K" found grateful recipients for the sweaters in athletic squads in Fostoria, Bowling Green and Maumee. Ostensibly this was a recruiting-oriented effort to win Klan support among young men in the years just prior to reaching adulthood.[108]

The auxiliary women's and children's Klan units, at least early on, expanded the influence of the Wood County Ku Klux Klan. These initiatives helped the Klan shift from being a just another organization into one of the most powerful political forces in the county during the 1920s.

5

THE PEAK OF THE WOOD COUNTY KU KLUX KLAN

O n the night of Monday, August 13, 1923, a group of three crosses was ignited on South Enterprise Street in the city of Bowling Green. In addition to the ritual cross burnings, an explosion occurred that "startled" and woke many members of the neighborhood on an otherwise quiet summer evening. The explosive device was so loud that buildings shook, and concerned residents phoned in dozens of calls to public safety officials.[109]

The physical placement and timing of the burned crosses is worth exploration. The area of South Enterprise where the incident occurred was in a heavily Catholic neighborhood, and the scene of this incident happened to be within a block of St. Aloysius Catholic Church as well three blocks from the meeting room of the local Knights of Columbus group, a fraternal organization frequently attacked by Klan leaders as "evidence" of a plot by militant Catholics to impose their political will on unsuspecting "100 Percent Americans."

The cross burnings also occurred the night before a primary election, suggesting that the demonstration may have been a form of political intimidation. While no individuals or groups officially claimed responsibility for this particular incident (the Klan admitted that rogue Klan members burned the crosses but denied any connection to the explosive device), the net result was increased tensions and a veritable war of words between Protestants and Catholics in the city of Bowling Green.

The 1923 elections in Ohio proved to be one of the high points of Klan political strength in the Buckeye State. Support from the Ku Klux Klan led to mayoral victories for candidates in cities such as Youngstown, Portsmouth, Akron and Toledo.[110] In the city of Middletown, an entire slate of Klan candidates won at the ballot box for the board of education and the city commissioner posts.[111]

Klan candidates fared especially well in eastern Ohio's Mahoning Valley, winning mayoral campaigns in the cities of Girard, Struthers, Youngstown, Warren and Niles.[112] In the glow of its numerous electoral successes, Klan officials boasted that the Buckeye State was home to over 700,000 members at the time of the 1923 elections.[113] Editors of the *New York Times* in 1923 chided politicians in the state of Ohio for "pursuing a policy of 'silence' in the face of the menace."[114]

Klan members in Wood County occupied a wide range of municipal and county positions during the group's prominence in the mid-1920s. Some political officeholders joined the Klan at some point after they became employed in elected or appointed positions, while Kluxers parlayed their Klan connections into lucrative and influential offices.

One of the early moves by the Wood County Klan was to organize an effort to close businesses on Sundays in Bowling Green. While the Klan did not advertise themselves as organizers of the unofficial "blue" movement, over three-fourths of the signatories were Klan members. Others likely agreed to close their businesses out of either philosophical agreement with the idea or under pressure from the group.

The greenhouse and florist shop owned by Klan members William and Harold Milnor. *Center for Archival Collections.*

The signers of the covenant vowed to close their businesses on Sunday as well as on all legal holidays. In addition, the signatories agreed to close their businesses at noon on Thursdays "during July and August, beginning at the week following the Fourth." Finally, signers of the agreement decided to also close their businesses at "6:30 each night, except Saturday, at which time we agree to close at 10:00 pm." Grocers were allowed to "stay open Saturday nights until all were served." Barbers were allowed an extra half hour on top of the above closing times, ostensibly to accommodate late visitors to their shops.[115]

KLAN MEMBERS IN COUNTY AND MUNICIPAL GOVERNMENT POSITIONS

Members of the Wood County Ku Klux Klan could be found in the highest offices of county government in the 1920s and 1930s. Kluxers at various times served as Wood County sheriffs and deputy sheriffs, Wood County commissioners, county judges, county engineers and county prosecutor. Klan members also served as local mayors, city council members, police officers, justices of the peace and village marshals.

In some cases local officials joined the Klan after they attained their political or administrative positions. Other individuals used their Klan connections as political springboards to join the ranks of the county's political elites.

Klan members occupied a wide variety of elected and appointed positions in the various county municipalities during the 1920s and

Political ad for Klan member Ray D. Avery. *From the* Wood County Republican.

RAY D. AVERY

Candidate for Republican Nomination for

PROSECUTING ATTORNEY

1930s. Ray D. Avery, for example, was the prosecuting attorney for Wood County, and he was coincidentally a charter member of the Wood County Ku Klux Klan.

One method used by members of the Wood County Klan to increase the organization's political power was utilizing the time-honored tradition of seizing control of party machinery at the grass-roots level. In Wood County, the Klan was overwhelmingly pro-Republican in orientation, and in the period from 1923 to 1926, many Klan members were elected to county Republican precinct chair positions.

By 1926, the Klan had unofficially gained control of the county Republican Party. Approximately 55 percent of precinct chairs were at one time Klan members, and many of the officers of the county party were Klansmen, including Chairman John E. Kelly and Vice-chairman Lester D. Hill.[116] Klan members thus composed a majority of Republican Party members from Wood County sent to the state convention in 1926 and 1928.

RAYMOND F. WITTE

Republican Candidate for Sheriff in Wood County

at the election November 2nd, 1926

Mr. Witte was born at Pemberville, O., 36 years ago and has been a resident of Wood County during his entire life, with the exception of four years in the United States Navy. Mr. Witte has been former Deputy Sheriff, two years as County Motor Cop and one year as first Deputy. Mr. Witte is a resident of Lake Twp. and promises if elected an able and efficient administration of the Sheriff's office.

Campaign ad for Raymond Witte, Wood County sheriff. *Wood County Republican.*

Despite the fact that at the national level the Ku Klux Klan was beginning to lose steam in 1926, in Wood County the November 1926 election showed that the organization was still influential. Wood County Klan members won several county commissioner seats plus the posts of county recorder and county treasurer.

In the 1926 election, the Klan also backed a winning candidate in a race that directly influenced one of their most cherished issues: Prohibition enforcement. Wood County voters elected Raymond F. Witte as county sheriff in this cycle, putting into office an individual who had been a dues-paying Klansman for at least three years prior to the November 2 election.

Witte was not alone in his status as a Wood County sheriff who had also been a Klan member. At least two other Wood County sheriffs who held the office between 1915 and 1945 at one point had been members of the Wood County Ku Klux Klan.

In keeping with the group's focus on public education as a means of achieving "100 Percent Americanism," it is not surprising that members of the Ku Klux Klan gravitated toward employment in public school systems during the 1920s and 1930s. Klan members could be found in a wide variety of roles in most of the public school systems in the county during the 1920s. These ranged from lower-level employees, such as teachers and maintenance staff, up to higher positions, including principals, superintendents and school board officials.

Klan members occupied many of the most important administrative positions in public school systems in Wood County in the 1920s. Chalmer B. Riggle[117] and John A. Nietz[118] both served as superintendents of Perrysburg Public Schools, and Roy A. Hammond served in a similar capacity in North Baltimore schools. Charles S. Harkness served as superintendent of the Wood County school system and as a member of the county board of education,[119] while Klan member Orin Clive Treece worked as a principal at Perrysburg High School.[120]

Klan member Harry O. Stout worked at Bowling Green High School as a science teacher for many years. Interestingly, Stout also served on a cooperative basis with Bowling Green State Normal College working with student teachers as they gained classroom experience as part of their education degrees.[121]

Like his fellow Klan member Harry Stout, teacher Elmer L. Boyles also worked at Bowling Green High School. Boyles served as a mathematics instructor for the district,[122] and he, too, worked to train student teachers in conjunction with Bowling Green Normal College.

Interestingly, Bowling Green State Normal College (later Bowling Green State University) did not seem to be an important focus for Klan recruiters. Cross-referencing Klan membership lists with student and employee names has revealed only two students and two maintenance workers as Klan members. Four Klan members in a college community of several thousand students, staff and faculty is a much lower percentage than comparisons with other segments of the population of Wood County.

Part of this statistical anomaly regarding the relative absence of Klan members on campus might be explained by the fact that any students who happened to be Klan members might have simply belonged to a klavern in their hometowns (setting aside the issue that the Klan had greater appeal to middle-aged persons with disposable income). More importantly, though, the primacy of the field of teacher education at the college likely meant that the Klan agreed with the mission of Bowling Green Normal College, as one of the key goals of the Klan was to increase the number and quality of public schools.

KLAN MEMBERS AS UNOFFICIAL LAW ENFORCEMENT FIGURES

One of the issues that galvanized early support for the Ku Klux Klan was the spike in criminal activity connected to Prohibition. The enactment of the Eighteenth Amendment and the Volstead Act produced unintended consequences, most notably the production and distribution of alcoholic beverages by criminal groups. The national Ku Klux Klan acknowledged that Prohibition provided the group with an unexpected membership boost: "Wherever the Ku Klux Klan operates it is a clear indication that some public officers, not necessarily all of them, have previously violated their oath of office in refusing to enforce the law."[123]

The Ohio legislature, in an effort to provide the mechanisms by which Prohibition could be enforced, passed legislation known as the Crabbe Act. This law provided compensation for mayors, law enforcement officials and certain judicial personnel for their efforts to enforce the ban on alcohol in Ohio, and the act also extended the already considerable powers of local officials to try cases. Most cities and towns in Ohio used a form of a mayor's court to hear cases related to Prohibition violations.[124]

Like many Klan chapters in the 1920s, the Wood County Klan sought to play a role in curbing Prohibition-related criminal activity. Some of this activity took the form of simply providing information about crime to local officials, while some Klan members took on semi-official roles as adjunct support personnel with law enforcement agencies. Some Klansmen, however, took matters in their own hands and engaged in vigilante action against purported criminals.

Klan members were among the "other members of the raiding party" who accompanied local, state and federal law enforcement officials on a highly publicized 1923 raid. The liquor raid resulted in the arrests of twelve persons from crimes ranging from "selling liquor," "furnishing liquor" and "giving away liquor." Klan members appeared to act primarily as undercover informants in the operation, but they were in fact armed and present the day of the twenty-man raid of various sites in Rossford.[125]

The efforts of Klan members to bolster the fight against violations of Prohibition laws were applauded by a number of members of the community. The editor of the *Prairie Depot Observer* noted that "hooded bands should not be necessary to enforce the laws, but the K.K.K. has done more to stop the bootlegger than all the paid officials in the land."[126] The *Wood County Republican* described the Klan's antibootlegging work as "terrorizing the lawbreaker with the fear of being detected."[127]

The Klan was instrumental in forming what became known as the Dry Federation. This coalition of members of the Ku Klux Klan, the Anti-Saloon League, the Woman's Christian Temperance Union and other supporters of Prohibition laws emerged in 1924 in Wood County. The purpose of the group was to assist the government "in every way in securing respect for the Prohibition law by seeing that it was rigidly enforced."[128]

During the peak years of the Klan in Wood County, the president of the Dry Federation was Klan member Dr. Charles B. Hatfield, a physician from Bloomdale. In the period from 1924–26, the other officers of the Dry Federation were also Klan members: James M. Beard of Portage and Reverend Paul J. Gilbert of Bowling Green.[129] Klan members and their wives also heavily populated the group's executive committee.

The Wood County Ku Klux Klan thus flexed its muscles in a wide variety of venues across the spectrum of political activity to advance its agenda. However, when united behind a political candidate, the Klan was capable of remarkable influence in individual elections.

SHOWDOWN
A Bitter Klan vs. Non-Klan Election

One of the earliest tests of the strength of the Wood County Klan occurred when the Reverend Rush A. Powell—a charter member of the local Klan klavern, a minister at Trinity United Brethren Church in Bowling Green and a regional administrator with the United Brethren Church—declared in July 1924 that he would run for a state senate seat. Powell was a newcomer to politics, having worked his entire adult life in ecclesiastical positions.

At the time of his announcement, the *Wood County Republican* lauded Powell in a front-page editorial as a "man of high character and ideals who at the same time has the mind and courage to make himself felt in the Ohio General Assembly." Reverend Powell, observed the editors, possessed the "worth, ability, capacity, and desire to serve his fellows." According to the editorial, Powell decided to run for state senate "because he was solicited by many staunch Republicans."[130]

What the *Wood County Republican* editors did not reveal in their ringing endorsement of Reverend Powell was that they, like Powell, were members of the Ku Klux Klan. The publisher, editor, reporters and even the printers were naturalized Kluxers. The publisher Harvey H. Sherer was a charter member of the Wood County Klan, and his sons Marshall and Glen—both of whom held important positions at the *Republican*—soon joined him as Kluxers. By 1924, the newspaper had evolved into a semiofficial mouthpiece for the county Klan, and the paper regularly offered the Klan front-page space for news about the group as well as for reprinted Klan propaganda from KKK newspapers and pamphlets.

The political campaign of Reverend Powell faced significant hurdles, not the least of which was the fact that Powell's Democratic opponent, Frank Thomas, had represented the Thirty-third Senate District of Ohio since 1916. In addition to his work in the Ohio Senate, Thomas also published a newspaper of his own, the *Wood County Democrat*. Prior to becoming a state senator, Thomas served as a member of the Ohio House of Representatives, the Bowling Green City Council and the Wood County Board of Tax Equalization.

Thus, the election was a showdown on many levels: Republican versus Democrat, Klan versus non-Klan and newspaper versus newspaper.

Powell and Thomas both ran unopposed and won their respective party nominations in the August 1924 primary. The two men began a heated campaign that would test the growing power of the Klan to influence county politics. Thomas made frequent use of his ownership of the *Wood County Democrat* to attack his opponent, especially related to the Reverend Powell's status as a Ku Klux Klan member. Interestingly, the *Democrat* did not break the story on the Powell-Klan connection, though Thomas may have tipped off other local papers. The *Democrat* denied making the accusation, arguing that "we took it for granted that the [*Bowling Green Sentinel-Tribune*] reporter knew what he was talking about" in reporting that the Reverend Powell was a Klansman.[131]

The *Democrat* in several issues took an almost taunting tone toward Powell in offering space in future editions of the paper for a rebuttal. The August 15, 1924 edition of the *Democrat* is typical of the efforts to bait Reverend Powell, and one can almost hear the smugness of Thomas and the *Democrat* staff in making an offer that they knew Reverend Powell could not accept, as this would betray his fellow Klansmen:

> *The* Democrat *had no intention to attack Rev. Powell as a citizen, but merely printed what the* Sentinel-Tribune *reporter had recorded. If Rev. Powell is not a member of the Klan, the columns of the* Democrat *are open to him for a denial of the report.*[132]

Thomas and the *Democrat* issued at least four such sarcastic offers to Reverend Powell in the ten weeks leading up to the November election. The strategy of linking the phrases "Reverend Powell" and "Ku Klux Klan" was also expanded to include placing several minor stories about the Klan next to innocuous news articles about Reverend Powell, such as a wedding announcement for his daughter being placed next to a story about a Klan gathering.[133]

Yet despite the leak of Reverend Powell's status as a member of the Wood County Ku Klux Klan, the November election demonstrated the political power of the KKK in the county. Powell garnered almost 75 percent of the vote in the election versus the Democratic incumbent, and while some credit for the landslide might go to the national GOP slate (Calvin Coolidge won in Ohio with 58.33 percent of the vote[134]), the thousands of Klan voters in Ohio's Thirty-third Senate District came out in droves for the minister-turned-senator.

The *Wood County Republican* addressed the issue of the role of the Klan during the election in a front-page editorial immediately following the election:

> *Rev. Rush A. Powell was overwhelmingly elected over Frank W. Thomas...*
> *This was no surprise as Thomas has been a candidate before and had held*

the offices of Representative and Senator both and did not prove satisfactory to the voters. He blames his defeat to the Klan, and it may be so, and it may be not.[135]

As a state senator, Powell served on a number of legislative committees, including Finance, Agriculture, County Affairs, Drainage and Irrigation and Soldiers' and Sailors' Homes. The *Wood County Republican* applauded his committee assignments, noting that "the fact that he has been given a place on the finance committee bespeaks the respect for which his colleagues have for his record as a financial manager of the U.B. church." Not surprisingly, given the interest that both Powell and the Klan had on prohibition enforcement, Reverend Powell was named chair of the Temperance Committee in the state senate.[136]

While serving in the state senate, Reverend Powell won another election in 1925, this time as conference superintendent of the United Brethren Church. Powell thus assumed much greater administrative duties, supervising churches across nearly one-third of the state of Ohio for the conference.[137]

At the peak of both his political and ecclesiastical careers, Reverend Powell apparently found that the workload was more than he could manage. In June 1926, right before the electoral filing deadline for the August primaries, Powell announced that he would not seek reelection to the state senate. The *Wood County Republican* reported that Powell "finds his new duties as superintendent so exacting that he has decided that justice to his work and to himself demands that he free himself from governmental duties."[138]

HARNESSING THE POWER OF THE KLAN TO PROMOTE BUSINESSES

One aspect of Klan life that appealed to business owners was the idea that the Ku Klux Klan—as an exclusive fraternal organization—could be used to improve the financial fortunes of members whose livelihood depended on retail sales. The Wood County Ku Klux Klan boasted as members some of the most visible and powerful business owners in the county.

Some Klan members who owned businesses preferred to keep their affiliation with the hooded order a secret out of fear of customer backlash. This would especially make sense for Klan members who owned businesses in communities with sizeable Catholic populations, such as Perrysburg, Rossford and Bowling Green.

Other Klan members, however, were quite open with broadcasting their affiliations to the public. George L. Myers opened a billiard hall in North Baltimore that promised patrons a "100 Percent Pool and Billiard Hall Parlor." In case readers missed the "100 Percent" hint, Myers added the phrase "100 Pct. American" at the bottom of the advertisement to reinforce the Klan slogan. The use of capital *K* letters in each corner made it highly unlikely that a reader could mistake the intent of the proprietor.

Advertising campaigns such as the "100 Percent Pool and Billiard Hall" opened by George Myers served purposes other than building sales through tapping into the potential economic power of Klan membership. Such an advertisement more

Top: The Commercial Bank in Bowling Green. *Center for Archival Collections*.

Right: "100 Percent American" pool hall advertisement. *From the North Baltimore Times*.

K ============================ **K**

AT LAST!

A

100 Percent

Pool and Billiard Parlor.

Newly Installed Tables and Modern Furniture and Equipment

Hotel Columbia

GEO. MYERS, Prop.

100 Pct. American

K ============================ **K**

subtly informed Catholics, African Americans and immigrants that they were not allowed in the establishment, serving as an informal method of segregation by religion, race and/or birth origin status.

An intriguing number of bank officials and bank employees joined the Wood County Ku Klux Klan in the 1920s. In particular, many Klan members could be found among the officers and boards of directors for the Bank of Wood County, the Commercial Bank & Savings of Bowling Green, and the State Bank of Bowling Green. The desire of these individuals to join the Klan might reflect concerns about crime in the community, or they may have viewed the Ku Klux Klan as another opportunity to network and develop bank business.

Business owners who were Klan members ranged from those who operated small retail establishments—like Fred Hale's newsstand in Bowling Green—to those who owned larger businesses, such as Gus Keller's freight line company. Klan members owned pharmacies, operated construction companies, ran consumer-related businesses and owned industrial firms like tile factories and electrical supply warehouses.

VIGILANTE KLAN ACTIVITY

Despite the efforts of the Ku Klux Klan to promote itself as a law-abiding organization, Klan members in Wood County occasionally took it upon themselves to engage in vigilantism. Local newspapers during the 1920s detailed a wide range of vigilante activities in the county, though the Wood County Klan often denied its involvement or attributed the extra-legal actions to rogue elements within the group.

The *North Baltimore Times* recounted a violent incident in which individuals who uttered disparaging comments at a memorial for the late president Warren G. Harding experienced a "near lynching." The two "radicals" were residents of New York City, described by the *Times* as "the hot-bed of foreign, radical, and bolshevist agitation." The angry crowd forced the couple into a vehicle and drove them into the countryside, where ropes were strung from a tree. The couple was spared when the man "begged to be allowed to kiss the flag," at which point the mob relented and warned the couple to leave the state.[139]

On the Wood-Seneca County line simmered a long-running dispute between regional Klan members and the publisher of the *Bettsville Taxpayer*,

Stanley Feasel, who was a Wood County resident in Liberty Township. As the name of the *Taxpayer* implies, this was an anti-tax publication that took a strident stand against the use of tax dollars for public education. Given the Klan's high degree of emphasis on public education as a means to "Americanize" immigrants and break up the perceived power of Catholic parochial schools, it is not surprising that Feasel would incur the wrath of the Klan.

Feasel's first altercation occurred in March 1923, when he received a threatening letter signed by the "Kansas K.K. Klan." Kansas Station was an unincorporated village several miles east of the county line, and the writer of the letter was angry about Feasel's stance against a tax levy for a new public school building. The letter also included a drawing of Feasel "being torn to pieces." Feasel told a correspondent from the *Prairie Depot Observer* that he "slept well last night" after the warning but added that "some of my friends are worried for my welfare."[140]

The culmination of the feud occurred when Feasel drove home from Tiffin, Ohio, on the evening of August 13, 1924. The *Bloomfield Derrick* reported that Feasel's vehicle was fired on by an unknown assailant, and the bullet "pierced the side of his automobile and missed hitting him by a few inches." Moments prior to the shooting the driver of a vehicle traveling in the opposite direction "had attempted to block the road," but Feasel averted the roadblock. Fragments of glass from the shattered window wound up in Feasel's shirt pocket.[141]

Klan members orchestrated a botched 1923 raid on a suspected gambling den in a news report printed in the *North Baltimore Times*. The Klan members in full regalia entered a Montpelier pool hall and went to the second-story rooms, where gambling was alleged to have occurred. In an attempt to catch the gamblers by surprise, the Klan members turned out the lights.

In the chaos that ensued, "shots rang out," and a bullet hit one of the gamblers. Three Klansmen were arrested for the incident, and one of the Klan members was charged with attempted murder. The Klansmen claimed that the Montpelier mayor and law enforcement officials endorsed the raid, described as an "action by the Klan and other public-spirited officials."[142]

Other vigilante actions by Wood County Klan members included the destruction of illegal stills and alcohol caches, physical intimidation and violence against suspected bootleggers and still operators and breaking into private property to investigate alleged liquor law violations. Newspapers hint at yet further vigilante actions, but illegal and extra-legal actions by a secret society are notoriously difficult to document. These individuals knew their actions could result in personal and organization legal problems that even highly placed friends might not be able to solve.

6

THE WOOD COUNTY
KU KLUX KLAN AS
PUBLIC SPECTACLE

The three robed and hooded Klansmen carried an eight-foot cross onto property owned by the Baltimore & Ohio Railroad. Earlier, the men covered the wooden cross with burlap and then doused the device with fuel oil. Upon reaching their destination, the men drove the wooden cross into the ground and set it ablaze before driving off in a waiting automobile.

The flames leapt into the night air of the small town of North Baltimore, Ohio, and the conflagration caught the attention of the railroad facility's night watchman as well as diners at a nearby restaurant. At the top of the cross was a tin plate that contained the inscription "K.K.K."

It is unclear who the Klansmen intended as the recipient of their message. The *Wood County Republican* noted that the Klan "has been active in attempting to eliminate the bootleggers,"[143] so perhaps the group knew of some nearby activity in the illegal alcohol trade. It is also possible that a group of transients had been living near the railroad yard and that the burning cross was an attempt by the Klan to terrorize migrants into leaving the area. Whatever the reasons for the placement of the flaming cross, the message was not missed by the citizens of Wood County. The Klan had arrived, and the group meant to impose its collective will on the area.

The Wood County Klan made significant use of highly visible activities during the 1920s. In part, this was simply publicity to build its membership rolls, as well as to provide visceral entertainment for members. However, activities such as cross burnings, Klonvocations, parades and church "visits" (derisively termed "invasions" by at least a few unhappy members of local churches) served as not-so-subtle terror tactics to keep anti-Klan forces at bay.

PUBLIC KLAN SPEAKERS AT OPEN MEETINGS

One of the most important recruitment tools used by the Wood County Ku Klux Klan was the use of large outdoor open meetings. The Klan utilized speakers from regional and national KKK circuits to provide curious residents of local communities an opportunity to hear the group's message in a more casual setting, and frequently Klan members and their family members from far away attended the event to create a larger crowd. Often these events included family-friendly social activities, such as band music, food concessions and games.

An outdoor Klan meeting on August 10, 1924, featured a speaker from the national headquarters of the Ku Klux Klan. The *Wood County Republican* reporter who attended the rally, held at a place known as Finney Grove, noted that "one thousand men attended" and that "five hundred automobiles lined the borders of the field." As a result of the meeting, "a goodly number of real men signed their intention of becoming a part of the movement."[144]

In the same week, similar outdoor meetings were held in Tontogany, Cygnet and Prairie Depot featuring national speakers. The *Wood County Republican* reporter observed that the meetings were "very satisfactory" and that "gratifying results" occurred in terms of recruiting potential members.[145]

A Klan event at Pemberville on September 12, 1923, brought a "mammoth crowd" to hear a national lecturer speak. The reporter for the *Wood County Republican* observed that "five hundred men," all of whom were "true Americans," inked their names to a charter sheet in the hopes of "becoming a part of the greatest movement ever attempted to protect the American home and school."[146]

The first public naturalization ceremony of the Wood County Klan took place on September 10, 1923, just outside the city North Baltimore. The *Wood County Republican* reported that "five hundred real American men took the oath of allegiance" that evening. The reporter also claimed that "one thousand Klansmen were in attendance" as both spectators and event security.[147] The event was capped off with the burning of three crosses, one of which was thirty feet in height, plus the burning of large wooden representations of the letters KKK.

The Klan staged a large public meeting in the village of Bloomdale on the evening of August 6, 1924, that—according to the correspondent for the *Bloomdale Derrick*—was the "biggest crowd in Bloomdale in a long time." The event resulted in heavy traffic, and a nearby fallow field "was filled full of automobiles besides the large number that were parked on the street." The event included a band playing popular music plus a refreshment tent with food, beverages and ice cream.[148]

CROSS BURNINGS

The ritualistic use of cross burnings by the Ku Klux Klan owes much to the influence of popular culture. There are no documented records of crosses being burned by the first wave of the Ku Klux Klan during Reconstruction, and it appears that the 1905 book *The Clansman* and the 1915 film *Birth of a Nation* served as the inspirations for the second wave of the Ku Klux Klan to take up the fiery cross.

The Klan that emerged during the decade of the 1920s had a problematic relationship with cross burnings. On one hand, a burning cross was an effective symbol of terror to opponents as well as a source of inspiration to some onlookers, especially new Klan members and potential Klan recruits. On the other hand, the burning of a cross also focused negative attention on the group from non-Klan local authorities and concerned citizens. The Klan would be forced to tread lightly with regard to cross burnings, alternating between wholeheartedly embracing the practice and occasionally denying the group's participation in the activity depending on the particular circumstances of a given cross burning event.

Frequently the Klan and its apologists would deny the group's involvement in cross burnings. After an August 1924 cross burning near a Catholic Church in Bowling Green, the editors of the pro-Klan *Wood County Republican* opined that the idea that the Klan was responsible for the incident was "positively pronounced an untruth" and that the burnt crosses were merely an attempt by Klan opponents to put "the organization in a more unfavorable light in the eyes of the public."[149]

Yet Klan denials of cross burnings are difficult to believe. The burning cross was a powerful symbol evoked in a wide variety of Klan literature and imagery. One need only look at the masthead of *The Fiery Cross*, a Ku Klux Klan newspaper with wide circulation in the 1920s. Not only did the Klan newspaper adopt as its name a variation of a burning crucifix, but the logo also included an image of a hooded Klan knight carrying a flaming torch. While Klan officials might not have authorized every burning cross, at the same time it is clear that individual Kluxers understood the power of the burning cross to terrorize perceived enemies.

Compare, for example, the coverage by the *Wood County Republican* of a cross burning that took place at midnight on Christmas Eve in 1923. The front-page article noted that "Christmas was ushered in by the burning of a 20-foot cross and the explosion of a number of aerial bombs" by approximately 150 Klan members. The Klan's holiday festival took place on Dixie Highway just north of the city of Bowling Green, where the Kluxers had gathered to "celebrate the breaking of Christmas morn."[150]

In both cases, cross burnings were accompanied by explosive devices, yet when there was significant concern expressed by local citizens about the first incident, the Klan quickly denied any involvement with the activity. Instead, unknown anti-Klan forces were accused of imitating Klan rituals to discredit the group, though it is difficult to identify a group other than the Klan that had a history of such activity.

Catholics in Bellevue were the target of a similarly threatening cross burning on April 9, 1923. A *North Baltimore Times* reporter noted that the fiery cross burned "in the sight of hundreds of shoppers" along Main Street. Of particular note is that the burning cross within fifty yards of both St. Augustine Church and the local Knights of Columbus. The incident auspiciously occurred, noted the *Times* reporter, on the "eve of the initiation of a large class of Knights of Columbus."[151]

One of the strangest—and perhaps most threatening—uses of the burning cross by the Wood County Klan took place on April 2, 1923. Klansmen ignited a burning cross on public school grounds in the town of Bloomdale after a performance of the operetta *Miss Cherry Blossom*.

The plot of the theatrical production involved a young American girl living in Japan whose parents died of an unidentified fever. The girl was brought up in a Japanese family not knowing of her true origins until later in life. While the production has an ending where the girl returns to America and marries a handsome young man, evidently anti-Japanese sentiments among Klan members were sufficiently intense that this plotline offended their sensibilities.

The cross burning took place after the performance, suggesting that the Klan intended people leaving the show to see the fiery crucifix. Klan members also left behind a silk flag after the performance, ostensibly as a not-so-subtle reminder that school officials ought to be focusing on "100 Percent American" themes in future theatrical productions.[152]

THE KLAN AND PUBLIC SCHOOLS

One of the principal concerns of the second wave of the Ku Klux Klan was the improvement and expansion of public schools. Klan ideology viewed public schools both as a counterweight to Catholic parochial schools and as a means to better assimilate immigrants. Public schools, Klan members believed, were the most important tool to promote and reinforce the values they associated with white Protestant nationalism.

One of the methods the Wood County Ku Klux Klan used to strengthen its connections with public schools was through the use of school visits by hooded and robed members. Typically these prearranged visits involved ritual and ceremonial activities to emphasize the sincerity and seriousness of the Klan, and most visits also included gifts to the school such as flags and Bibles.

Klan visits to schools served an additional purpose, namely that of publicity for the group. Children certainly would have recounted the visits to their parents upon returning home from school, and parents—whether outraged by the visit or sympathetic to the Klan cause—would have naturally discussed the incidents with family members, neighbors and co-workers.

The *Perrysburg Journal* reported on a December 5, 1923 Ku Klux Klan visit to Perrysburg High School. Students were attending a morning religious service in the school chapel when "they were somewhat surprised and awe-stricken" by the arrival of a contingent of Klan members to the service.[153]

The eight hooded and robed Klansmen staged a procession down the aisle where they were greeted by Chalmer B. Riggle, superintendent of Perrysburg Public Schools. In addition to a "good sized Holy Bible," the Klan presented the school with an eight-by-twelve-foot American flag. After singing the patriotic song "America," the Klansmen processed silently out of the chapel.[154]

As was the case with similar church visits by Klan members, often the visits by Klansmen to public schools were enabled by insiders. In the case of the Perrysburg High School incident in 1923, fellow Klan member Chalmer B. Riggle likely played a role in arranging the visit, and he also presumably helped arrange similar Klan visits to Perrysburg schools in 1924.

Ku Klux Klan members visit Perry School to present a gift of the American flag, 1928; this is one of the few surviving photographs of the Wood County Klan. *Center for Archival Collections.*

About fifteen Klan members posed with the students and staff of the school for the photographer on the chilly morning. The Klan presented school officials with a flag and a Bible, and they participated in a ceremony in which the three-by-five-foot American flag was unfurled and raised on the flagpole. Klan members led the students and staff in a brief prayer before marching in procession back to their automobiles.

KLAN FUNERALS

The death of a Klansman provided the Klan with a different type of publicity opportunity. Klan members frequently used funerals as occasions for displaying Klan regalia and creating elaborate processions through the communities in which the group operated.

One such Klan funeral occurred with the death of Howard L. Homes, a railroad worker from Toledo who was crushed by a locomotive. Homes lived long enough to request that his body be transported to his boyhood home in Arcadia, Ohio, a town just south of the Wood County border.

Hundreds of Klan members from Toledo traveled in eighty-two vehicles, according to the reporter from the *Wood County Republican*. At the Wood County line they were joined by a large contingent of Wood County Kluxers, and later, Klan members from the city of Findlay joined in a funeral procession that was "three miles in length." The procession included a performance by the Toledo Klan band.[155]

The *North Baltimore Times* reported a Klan grave visitation that occurred in the town of Bettsville on May 21, 1923. Eight Klansmen traveled across the county line to the Old Fort Cemetery to pay tribute to a fallen Klan comrade who had died of unidentified causes a week earlier. The Klan delegation marched into the cemetery carrying an American flag and a cross covered with red roses. The Kluxers planted the cross at the "foot of the grave, kneeling and praying silently and spreading carnations on the mound."[156]

Members of the Wood County KKK staged a more elaborate Klan funeral in North Baltimore for Harold L. Jones, a nineteen-year-old man who "was taken from this earth suddenly Friday noon while conversing with his mother." Jones, according to the *North Baltimore Times*, "had only been a member of the Klan for a short time but had made himself felt as a true American citizen during his membership." Klan members provided the ceremony with a "beautiful Fiery Cross floral piece" as part of their collective condolences. The *North Baltimore Times* account described the efforts by the Klan members to memorialize their fallen comrade:

> *The Klansmen gathered in the southern part of the cemetery, and after all ceremonies were performed, marched with silent tread, arms folded (masked and robed) each one carrying a white carnation, after gathering around the grave the members knelt in silent prayer for a short time, then arose and with outstretched hand paused a moment, then deposited the carnations on the grave. This done, they returned as silently as they came, disrobed, and returned to their homes, mourning the loss of so young a life, but all with one thought in mind: "God's will be done."*[157]

Funerals for deceased Klansmen served several purposes for the Wood County Klan. The presence of Klan members at the graveside or funeral home reinforced the idea that the Klan was a benevolent fraternal organization dedicated in part to assisting the families of Klansmen in times of need. The public demonstration of solemnity helped communicate the strong religious character of the Klan, perhaps mitigating in the eyes of some spectators the strong white supremacist views of the group. Finally, Klan funerals helped perpetuate the idea that the Ku Klux Klan was a powerful group that seemed to influence every aspect of American life.

KLAN THEATRICAL PRODUCTIONS

One of the more unusual public spectacles sponsored by the Wood County Ku Klux was a December 1924 theatrical production entitled *The Martyred Klansman*. The show was a three-act play based on a piece of Klan propaganda by the same name that was loosely based on the death of a Klan member during a riot in Carnegie, Pennsylvania.

COME! SEE!

"THE MARTYRED KLANSMAN"

BY G. F. CARR
That Great American Dramatic Play in 3 Acts

Del-Mar Theatre
BOWLING GREEN, OHIO
DECEMBER, 18 - 19

Mixed Chorus. Special Orchestra Selection

ADMISSION $1.00

NO RESERVATIONS   COME EARLY

Doors Open at 7:30 P. M.   Show Starts at 8:30 P. M.

Eastern Standard Time

Under Auspices Wood County Relief Association

Advertisement for the "Martyred Klansman." *From the* Wood County Republican.

96

The script for the production was written by a Marion, Ohio Klansman named G.F. Carr. A small traveling troupe of Klan actors served as the core for the cast of characters, and a handful of local Klansmen had roles as extras.

The Klan benefited from having additional connections in the entertainment industry. The owner and manager of the Del-Mar Theatre in Bowling Green was Clark M. Young, who joined the Klan at the beginning of 1924. The Del-Mar facility was also used for numerous larger Klan events over the next two years in the mid-1920s.

Young's participation in the Klan was likely a precarious one, given the denunciations that the Klan frequently levied against what the group termed the "Jew-owned entertainment industry." Perhaps Young enthusiastically embraced Klan ideology, but it is equally likely that Young decided that joining the Klan was a way to avoid having his theater threatened by angry Klansmen should his theater end up showing a film that the Klan found immoral or offensive.

The Klan booked the show for two nights, and advertisements indicated that proceeds from the event would benefit a Klan charity known as the Wood County Relief Association. Unfortunately, due to "the closeness to Christmas," as well as "the extremely wet weather on Thursday night turning to very cold on Friday night," the number of people who attended the show fell far below the expectations of Klan organizers.[158]

CHURCH INVASIONS

One of the most effective public tactics used by the Wood County Klan was the use of church visits, derisively referred to as church "invasions" by opponents. Typically, a group of hooded Klansmen entered a particular church in the middle of a service and publicly presented the church with a "gift," usually in amounts between twenty and fifty dollars. Many times the Klan would prearrange such visits with the minister, though sometimes these visits were unannounced.

A 1923 Ku Klux Klan visit to the Rudolph Church of Christ was typical of the format for church spectacles involving Klansmen. Just before the sermon by Reverend C. Faun Leiter, a small group of hooded Klan members silently entered the church and marched in procession down the aisle. The Kluxers were met at the lectern by Reverend Leiter, who accepted a fifty-dollar cash donation. The Klan members departed the church after leading the congregation in a short Bible reading and prayer.

Reverend Leiter, it should be added, had become a Klan member by at least January 1924, and if he was not officially a member before the Klan visit, he certainly was sympathetic to their cause, at least in the version of the event printed by the *Wood County Republican*. In his sermon, Reverend Leiter discussed the "good works" that the Ku Klux Klan had been engaged in, and he urged members of the congregation to consider membership in the organization.[159]

Some Klan church visits deviated from the prototype, however, and the term "invasion" better fits some Ku Klux Klan spectacles. Such was the case with the August 5, 1923 Klan visit to the African Methodist Episcopal Church in Circleville. A group of twenty-five hooded Klansmen entered the church during services, marched up the aisle and gave the minister twenty dollars before exiting the church. The invading Klansmen created "much consternation among the dusky folk present," according to the *North Baltimore Times*.[160]

Klan visits to religious facilities associated with African Americans, Catholics, immigrants and/or Jews served several purposes. On one level,

K.K.K. Gives Money to Negroes

25 hooded Klansmen donated $30 to the African Methodist church at Circleville Sunday evening and $20 to the minister, after having marched down the church aisles during services and creating much consternation among the dusky folk present.

A 1923 headline highlighting KKK visit to a black church. *From the* North Baltimore Times.

this was a somewhat ham-fisted attempt to counter charges that the Klan was a group that promoted hate; after all, if Klansmen hated those who were not white native-born Protestants, why would they give their heard-earned money to these supposed enemies?

Yet clearly a Klan visit to a religious space—such as the Circleville African Methodist Episcopal Church—served a more sinister purpose. Klan members were communicating that they were a force to be reckoned with and that they had claimed for themselves the right to invade even the most sacred spaces of others in order to promote their own views. Given the "consternation" among African Americans observed by the reporter for a newspaper sympathetic to the Klan like the *North Baltimore Times*, Klan members undoubtedly used these "alien" church visits as a method of intimidating other groups.

KLAN KLONKLAVES

One of the most important public events in the operation and maintenance of a Klan chapter was its participation in large formal KKK meetings. The Wood County Klan referred to these events as "Klonklaves," though the term has alternately been spelled "Konklave" or "Konclave." Typically, these involved hundreds and sometimes thousands of members from several regional Klan chapters.

The first official Klonklave that can be documented in Wood County occurred on October 4, 1923. The KKK used the Wood County Fairgrounds as the staging area for the event. The highlight of the evening was a parade that passed through the streets of the city of Bowling Green, and at the front of the parade were a pair of Klan marching bands.[161] The *Wood County Republican* described the size of the parade as "mammoth," while the *Wood County Democrat* estimated the number of hooded Klansmen in the parade at 500 marchers.[162] A reporter for the *Daily Sentinel-Tribune* estimated the number of parade participants at as many as 660 people, using a mathematical formula that incorporated a four-mile-per-hour parade speed and the average distance between marchers.[163]

It is interesting to note that the parade route traveled straight through the neighborhood with the heaviest concentration of Catholic residents. Undoubtedly, this was a provocation to local Catholics, especially given the

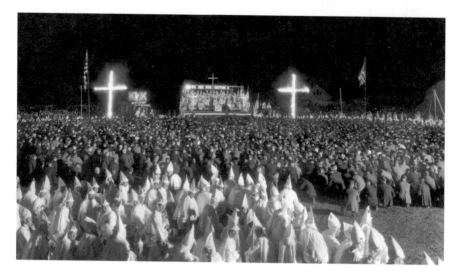

A 1923 Ku Klux Klan klonclave. *Ohio Historical Society.*

fact that the parade passed directly in front of St. Aloysius Church and also the meeting place of the Bowling Green Knights of Columbus.

The October 4, 1923 Klonklave attracted people from a wide geographical area. The *Daily Sentinel-Tribune* reporter spoke with attendees from Toledo, Findlay, Wapakoneta, Napoleon, Lima, Defiance, Bryan and Tiffin as well as other cities. Approximately "210 machine loads" of visitors came from Findlay alone.[164]

The Wood County KKK held its first major outdoor Klonklave with regional attendance on May 6, 1924. The event occurred on a Tuesday evening, and the reporter from the *Wood County Republican* noted that the meeting was a "mammoth gathering from all over this section of the state" and that three hundred Knights were naturalized in the ceremony. New Klan initiates walked between a lengthy row of hundreds of hooded Knights on the left and a line of "red fire" on the right, creating a sort of human-flame gauntlet for the candidates to walk as they approached the stage. Klan chapters from several counties were represented at the event.[165]

The Wood County Klan hosted one of the largest Klonklaves in the history of the state of Ohio on Saturday, October 24, 1924. The Klan hosted its 1924 Klonklave at the Wood County Fairgrounds in Bowling Green, and thousands of members of Klan chapters from Ohio, Indiana and Michigan attended the massive event. Curious onlookers from around the city and county enlarged the size of the crowds.

The *Wood County Republican* estimated that "from fifteen to twenty thousand persons" took part in the festivities. To put this into perspective, the crowd was one-third to one-half the total population of the county at the time, at least if the newspaper accounts can be taken at face value. The weather was "an ideal October night," and the *Republican* reporter suggested that this contributed to the large crowd size.[166]

The highlight of the Klonklave was a large parade that started at the fairground racetrack and wound its way through the streets of Bowling Green. The *Republican* reporter observed that "nearly a thousand men and women members of the Ku Klux Klan were in the parade, which was half a mile long." The parade was headed by three horsemen who were followed by the Toledo Klan Band as well as a Klan drum corps composed of Rossford and Toledo Kluxers.[167] Interestingly, the parade route did not take a confrontational route through Catholic neighborhoods; it is unclear if this was a decision made by the Klan or by the city of Bowling Green.

The death of famed politician and lawyer William Jennings Bryan provided the Wood County Klansmen with a reason to stage a well-attended public event in late July 1925. Bryan, who was not a Klan member at any time, nonetheless found himself praised by the Klan due to his efforts to defeat an anti-Klan plank at the 1924 Democratic National Convention.

As a result of this stance on the anti-Klan resolution, which Bryan believed to be a divisive and politically controversial position, he became the object of near veneration by Klansmen. The *Wood County Republican* described Bryan as "the greatest Klansman of our times," claiming that Bryan "stood for what was right the same as all honorable Klansmen do and will to the end of eternity."[168]

The large crowd that turned out for the Bryan memorial service gathered at "the Les Swindler farm north of the city" of Bowling Green on July 31, 1925. The Klan burned a cross and a Klan band played the song "Taps" for the late politician. The Reverend George Sesious of Findlay delivered a "fine eulogy" for Bryan to the gathered Klansmen and visitors.[169]

The efforts of members of the Wood County Klan to promote the organization via public spectacle certainly aided the group in its recruitment drives. At the same time, though, such activities also strengthened the resolve of anti-Klan forces while alienating some county residents who might not have otherwise formed negative opinions on the Klan.

7

RESISTANCE TO
THE WOOD COUNTY
KU KLUX KLAN
ㄴ

Reverend Nelson B. Martin of the Prairie Depot Church of Christ announced to his congregation on June 17, 1923, that there would be a surprise visitor for the following Sunday's evening service. Members of the congregation should "expect to have a speaker present who is a stranger to many of you." Reverend Martin hinted that "a crowd will greet him" when the speaker arrived at the church.[170]

Reverend Martin did not inform his congregation in the announcement that he was a Klan member and that the "special guest" was a recruitment agent for the Wood County Ku Klux Klan.

Unfortunately for Reverend Martin, word of the Klan visit leaked out, and outraged members of the congregation attempted to use physical force to prevent the arriving Klansmen and recruitment speaker from entering their church during the Sunday evening service on June 24, 1923. The planned meeting occurred, albeit with reduced attendance, and in apparent retaliation to anti-Klan members of the church, the Klan burned a cross and set off an explosive device outside the church at approximately 10:00 p.m. on Wednesday, June 27.[171]

It is perhaps not surprising that one week later, the church board announced the resignation of Reverend Martin as minister of the Prairie Depot Church of Christ.[172]

The Knights of the Ku Klux Klan did not meet with universal approval in the 1920s in Wood County, Ohio. Resistance to the group's recruiting efforts and public activities was at times somewhat sporadic, but an analysis of government records and newspapers from the decade reveals significant opposition to the Klan by residents of Wood County.

Part of the reason for the less intense opposition to the Klan in Wood County was simply a general lack of awareness of the group's connection to violence in post–Civil War history. School textbooks and history courses typically did not cover topics such as lynchings and other terror-related activities of the Klan during Reconstruction, and as discussed earlier, some forms of American popular culture actually glorified the Ku Klux Klan.

In addition, to some casual observers at the time, the Ku Klux Klan was just the latest in a long series of fraternal organizations in the county. The Klan's emphasis on structured hierarchy, exotic rituals, organizational secrecy and social gatherings may have seemed—at least to the uninitiated— not particularly different from those of fraternal groups such as the Masons, Woodsmen, Elk, Moose or Odd Fellows.

Certainly, Klan propaganda worked favorably to limit criticism and opposition to the group. In the case of Wood County, the Klan benefited from having virtual control over one of the local newspapers, the *Wood County Republican*, as the publisher, editor, reporters and even the printer of the paper were Klansmen. It appears that by March 1923 *Republican* owner Harvey Sherer was at least extremely sympathetic to the Klan, and at some point in that year, Sherer became one of the Wood County Klan's charter members. Several other newspapers in Wood County, especially the *North Baltimore Times* and the *Perrysburg Journal*, frequently ran articles that placed the Klan in a positive light.

Finally, the role of terror and intimidation as tools to reduce direct resistance to the Klan cannot be ignored. Church visits—termed "invasions" by some irritated parishioners—suggested that even the most sacred religious spaces were not free from the influence of the Klan. Cross burnings directly communicated the potential for violence inherent in the Klan, and public spectacles such as Klan parades, Klan funeral possessions and outdoor Klonvocations demonstrated the numerical power that the county Klansmen held.

The newspaper that consistently demonstrated antagonism toward the Klan was the *Wood County Democrat*. This newspaper frequently ran editorials expressing contempt of Wood County Kluxers, and news stories covering Klan-oriented events tended to either mock the participants or sound rhetorical alarms to the community about the dangers of the Klan.

In the January 19, 1923 edition of the *Wood County Democrat*, the newspaper printed an article on a speech by the Reverend John Cavanaugh, former president of the University of Notre Dame. The paper quoted Cavanaugh

Safe opened by burglars. *Center for Archival Collections.*

about what he referred to as the "anarchy of religious bigotry" in reference to the Ku Klux Klan. The Klan, according to Cavanaugh, seemed to have "derived its name from a stuttering idiot and its principles from an unfragrant [sic] voodoo philosophy."[173]

The *Democrat* ridiculed Klan participants in a vigilante action designed to track down would-be burglars of a bank in the village of Cygnet. A small posse of Klansmen stood watch over the bank until repairs could be made to its safe, and Klan volunteers—though ultimately unsuccessful in capturing the burglars—assisted the county sheriff in hunting the criminals.

The *Wood County Democrat* reporter, however, could not resist poking fun at the Kluxers, derisively inventing nicknames and suggesting that the Klan members were not the heroes they claimed to be:

> *Never again will the writer of this column speak slightingly of the Cygnet Klan…in this battle, "Clissy" is said to have covered himself with glory (and mud) by falling out of the path of a small cannonball shot by one of the robbers. "Cappy" performed the remarkable stunt of making himself thinner than the body of a four-inch sapling in protecting himself from the*

bullets. Earl Adams…proved to the world he is a brave man by arming himself with two young cannons and guarding the bank through Friday night, and Secretary Callan, not to be outdone in bravery, worked in the post office this week, right where the robbers' guards were giving battle to the citizens.[174]

Klan leaders frequently expressed a sort of perplexed shock at the animosity that their organization fostered in Klan opponents. Whether this response was feigned or genuine—or some combination of the two—the rhetorical reaction inevitably fell back to depicting the group as misunderstood by its opponents.

The *North Baltimore Times* reported that a traveling actor known for Broadway roles addressed a 1923 gathering at the Knights of Columbus. John F. Webber spoke at a luncheon organized by the group, and he discussed the fate of "Catholics, Hebrews, and Negroes" who served in the First World War. While not directly naming the Klan as the object of his condemnation, it is clear that the KKK was among the groups Webber included in this speech.

American veterans, argued Webber, were entitled to return home to a country grateful for their willingness to serve the country during wartime. Instead, Catholics, Jews and African Americans found that "the poison of hate and prejudice held sway." Hate mongering fanatics like Klansmen, Webber argued, gave "no heed to the great commandment in the Bible beneath their arms: 'Love thy neighbor as thyself.'"[175]

Hints at growing resistance to the Klan can be discovered in some of the group's propaganda. A 1924 editorial in the pro-Klan *Wood County Republican*—highly likely to have been penned by a Wood County Klan member—noted that whenever "a secret order of Protestant Americans tries to hold a peaceable open-air meeting, it automatically becomes the target for abuse, ridicule, brick bats, and bullets." The author sarcastically argued that "you would think from the actions of the opponents of this order that the Klan is a combination of man-eaters out to dine on Catholics, Jews, and negroes."[176]

The local Klan chapters faced vigorous anti-Klan opposition at a Klonklave held in the city of Fremont on May 24, 1924. Fremont is about thirty miles east of Bowling Green across the county line, and the Wood County Klan made up a significant amount of the "2,000 unmasked robed Klansmen" parading through the streets of the city. In particular the hundreds of Klan members in eastern Wood County were just a short drive from Fremont, and newspaper accounts documenting the event note the heavy presence of the Wood County KKK.

During the parade the Klansmen were confronted by some "unpatriotic American citizens" who made it "difficult for those parading to take the obscene language that was handed out." Even worse, the "anti-Americans and others began to throw rotten eggs at them on the edge of town." The pro-Klan *Wood County Republican* editorialized that the "egg brigade did not have the nerve to attack the front ranks of the parade" and that the protesters used a hedge for cover because they were "cowards."[177]

One of the difficulties in documenting resistance to the Klan is that the Klan itself worked hard to limit exposure of successful anti-Klan activities, most likely out of a fear of being perceived less powerful. It is apparent from editorials in the Wood County Republican, though, that numerous public Klan meetings faced significant resistance, up to an including attempts to shut down Klan events.[178]

One Klan-backed meeting that was successfully broken up by protesters involved a speaker from Toledo, Helen Jackson, who toured on Klan circuits as an "escaped nun." Jackson would recount dubious stories of infanticides in convents, physical and sexual abuse, torture and poison of nuns and other salacious tales intended to discredit the Catholic Church.[179]

The *Republican* declared that police "committed an outrage on the free American people" when they stepped in and ended Jackson's speech. Protesters had successfully pressured local officials into enforcing fire code regulations in the packed hall, and Jackson was later arrested for disorderly conduct when she continued her rant against the Catholic Church outside the hall.[180]

While many non-Klan politicians were reluctant to openly attack the KKK, a few political candidates directly denounced the Klan. The *North Baltimore Times* reported that a 1923 candidate for village marshal, Perry Weber, "tossed his glove in the face of the hooded order" in his political campaign. Weber, unlike his Klan-backed opponent, vowed that "when he makes an arrest he wants the prisoner to know who he is," unlike his presumably masked counterpart.[181]

A few Klan "visits" to local churches in Wood County did not meet with the enthusiasm for which KKK members had hoped. The Klan attempted to enter a Fostoria church, but the Reverend Wilford Lyons "refused to sanction the use of a mask in the church." The rest of the Klan members waited outside, and one unmasked Kluxer walked into the church; gave the minister a cash donation, a Bible and an American flag; and walked out. However, the *North Baltimore Times* noted that a "short time after the presentation a cross was burned outside of the church," suggesting that

Klan members were less than pleased about being instructed to remove their masks by Reverend Lyons.[182]

The *Daily Sentinel-Tribune* reported a similar reprimand of a Klan invasion by a member of the clergy at a Methodist church in October 1923. A group of "nine hooded and robed members of the Ku Klux Klan" interrupted the Sunday evening sermon of a Methodist minister named Francis McConnell. The minister not only refused the cash offering proffered by the Klansmen, but also chastised the group for arriving at a religious meeting "with masks on your faces." Moreover, declared Reverend McConnell, the Klansmen "have no right to interrupt a religious service."[183]

THE WOOD COUNTY KLAN'S PARTICIPATION IN THE NILES RIOT

Wood County Klan members were present at one of the most notorious and violent confrontations between Klan members and anti-Klan forces. The events took place in and around the city of Niles, Ohio, over the course of several months in 1924.

The city of Niles in eastern Ohio's Mahoning Valley had been an area of significant conflict between chapters of the Ohio Ku Klux Klan and anti-Klan forces. The city and surrounding areas were heavily Catholic, with large numbers of persons with Irish and Italian heritage. Klan leaders in Ohio had long viewed with alarm the "un-American" tendencies of residents of the Mahoning Valley. The KKK also noted that some individuals in the anti-Klan movement had connections to bootlegging, and they used this information in an attempt to add moral legitimacy to their campaigns in Niles and the surrounding areas.

The animosity generated by public Klan displays in the region boiled over in Niles in May 1924 during a Klan parade. Angry local residents knocked down a burning cross at the high school, and Klan members were pelted with rocks and bricks, and several shots were fired by unknown gunmen.[184]

In response to the disrupted parade, Klan officials put out a call to state and regional Klan members for a major Konklave to be held in Niles on June 21, 1924. Event organizers confidently predicted a Kluxer turnout of fifty thousand knights, but perhaps ten thousand Klan members made the journey to Niles.[185] This second major Klan event met with even greater resistance from local opponents of the Klan, and Klan officials were forced to call off the June 21 Konklave due to the rioting associated with the cancelled Klan event.

Tensions in the Mahoning Valley remained high between Klan and anti-Klan forces in the summer of 1924. There were sporadic violent incidents between the two groups, and regional Klan opponents coalesced into an umbrella group they called the Knights of the Flaming Circle, which adopted the use of a gasoline-soaked burning tire as a symbol to counter the Klan's burning cross. The mayor of Niles enacted a ban on public parades for a month to try to cool off the warring factions, but he inexplicably lifted the ban and issued a permit for the Klan to march in Niles on November 1, 1924.

Klan members around the state began to make preparations for the event. The Klan fervor was especially fueled by speeches given by C.A. Gunder, a charismatic Klan Kleagle who urged Klan members to defend their honor in light of the "injustices" suffered by the Niles Klan. Gunder chastised Klan members, sarcastically arguing that Kluxers "were a fine lot for letting a bunch of Wops scare you out." While state Klan leaders officially urged Klan members to obey the law, many frustrated Klan members began to consider extra-legal measures to rein in perceived lawlessness by Irish and Italian factions.[186] Tensions were further raised in the city when the home of the pro-Klan mayor was bombed by unknown assailants on October 29.

Among the attendees at the Niles Konklave on November 1, 1924, were "nine brave and fearless Klan members from Wood County,"[187] according to the pro-Klan *Wood County Republican* newspaper. From the newspaper account, it appears that the group of Klansmen principally drove along what would become U.S. 20, though the road did not bear that official designation until 1926. The group traveled from Bowling Green to Fremont, then took a Clyde-Norwalk-Medina-Kent route and finished with a Warren-to-Niles leg on the journey.

According to the *Republican*, Wood County Klan members were told that they would be "knocked off" by Italian gunmen if they attempted to make it to Niles and that their mission was "suicide." The parade, the Wood County Kluxers were told, was fraught with danger, as "the Italians had imported thousands of gunmen." The Klansmen, according to the newspaper account, "all the time were being watched by the dagoes in little squads."[188]

Coverage of the Niles riot by the *Republican* was highly sympathetic to the Klan cause. According to the paper, the planned Klan parade was much more than a mere public spectacle to city dwellers: "Protestant residents of Niles told the visitors that if this Klan parade was not carried out they would have to move out of Niles, as the Dago foreigners were so mean and dangerous they could not live there."[189]

The *Republican* reporter claimed that "none of the Klan members were armed when they went to Niles," but most contemporary accounts from the event indicate that many of the approximately one thousand Klan members who made it to the staging grounds brought firearms with them. Interestingly, in the next paragraph the *Republican* account acknowledged that "the Klan grounds were guarded by sworn in armed men at all times." Later in the news story, the reporter noted that the "first trouble started" when a carload of Klan members from Youngstown was stopped by "two disciples of Hades" and a Klan member fired a pistol in self-defense.[190]

City officials in Niles canceled the Klan parade in light of the impending showdown between Klan and anti-Klan forces. At the Klan grounds on the edge of the city of Niles, an "announcement came that troops had arrived and the city was under martial law." The Wood County Klan contingent was "not allowed to leave until six [p.m.] as the enemies had all the roads guarded to do harm to anyone attempting to come in or leave the city."

In spite of the widespread gunfire during the eighteen hours in which Klan and anti-Klan forces battled, only 12 people were injured in the rioting, and no one was killed. A total of 104 people were indicted for their roles in the fighting, most of whom paid small fines after pleading guilty to misdemeanors.[191]

Only three defendants spent any significant time in prison, and all of the Wood County Klan members returned safely home.

Yet despite the significant opposition to the Ku Klux Klan in Wood County, resistance alone could not bring an end to the power of the white supremacist group. The Klan in Wood County proved to be rather resilient in the face of antagonism, and other forces would ultimately prove to be more damaging to the KKK in Wood County than anti-Klan opponents.

8

DECLINE OF THE WOOD COUNTY KU KLUX KLAN

The flames from the burning building "poured through the roof like the flames of a huge blast furnace, piercing high in the air."[192] The intensity of the blaze on September 29, 1926, forced Bowling Green firefighters to request assistance from fire departments in Tontogany, Perrysburg and even Toledo.

The conflagration that engulfed the Del-Mar Theater—a building once known as the Opera House—also resulted in the destruction of a newsstand, an auto dealership, a hardware store, a tire store and the Bowling Green interurban railway station. Estimates of the losses due to the fire and damage from falling debris to nearby buildings exceeded $150,000, an amount equivalent to perhaps $2 million in the early twenty-first century.

Yet the "tongues of red flame that shot through the roof" of the Del-Mar destroyed more than merely a half dozen thriving businesses. The Wood County Ku Klux Klan regularly made use of the Del-Mar Theater for meetings and events, undoubtedly thanks to the active participation in the Klan by theater owner and manager Clark M. Young.

Harvey Sherer, publisher of the *Wood County Republican* and a charter member of the Wood County Klan klavern, summed up the feelings that many Klan members likely shared after the destruction of their favorite meeting place. The Del-Mar, Sherer opined in an editorial, was "shrouded with a romantic past unrivalled by any other pile of stone or wood for miles around."[193] Sherer mourned, among other events hosted at the Del-Mar, the numerous "home talent" minstrel shows produced at the theater. The

The charred ruins of Del-Mar Theater in Bowling Green, 1926. *Center for Archival Collections.*

Wood County Ku Klux Klan, as a result of the destruction of the Del-Mar Theater, lost its spiritual home.

The fortunes of the Ku Klux Klan in Ohio began to show signs of weakening at the halfway point of the 1920s, mirroring a nationwide trend. In large measure, this was due to highly public scandals involving Klan leaders, not the least of which was the second-degree murder conviction of David Curtis "D.C." Stephenson, the grand dragon of the Great Lakes region. The Ku Klux Klan lost a significant amount of member approval due to the criminal behavior of its own leadership.

Pro-Klan newspapers in Wood County offered little coverage of the Stephenson trial. The case brought a brief condemnation at the end of the editorial section from the *Wood County Republican*, which made efforts to describe the incident as the "isolated" work of a rogue Klan member. The *North Baltimore Times* simply said that an "ex-Klan leader has been found guilty of second degree murder with [a] lengthy prison sentence ahead of him."[194]

At the state level, internal strife and factional splits contributed to the decline of the Klan. Part of the internal fracturing of the Klan had its roots in the long-standing legal fight over control of the Klan between Joseph E. Simmons and Hiram Evans. The *North Baltimore Times* reported in January 1924 that Simmons sent representatives to the Buckeye State to gauge support for a new Klan-like fraternal organization. One envoy sent by

Simmons, a man named H.A. Lutz, called the Ohio Ku Klux Klan "rotten to the core," and he told two thousand assembled Klansmen that "either the Ohio Klan must be cleaned up, or it will shortly be faced by the organization of a new body in this state which will drive it out of existence."[195]

Internal strife even caused defections among Klan leadership in Northwest Ohio. The *Wood County Democrat* reported in early 1925 that a former Klan Kleagle responsible for recruiting in Wood County left the organization and engaged in a campaign of vilification against the Klan. W.E. Cahill spoke in front of a large crowd about the corruption in the Klan. Cahill claimed that he observed "such thievery and rascality [in the Klan] as will make your hair stand," adding that he personally witnessed Klan members carrying machine guns in parades "by the order of high officers." Cahill also hinted that Klan officials engaged in "white slavery" and that some members were willing to "cut the throats" of enemies, perhaps eerily foreshadowing the criminal trial of D.C. Stephenson later that year.[196]

In addition, gradually improving economic conditions in some parts of the state certainly contributed to the decline of the Klan in Ohio. While rural Ohio never reached the economic heights of the so-called Roaring Twenties enjoyed by larger urban centers, the financial well-being of Ohio agriculturalists had at least somewhat stabilized by mid-decade.

Some of the "threats" to mainstream white American values identified by Klan organizers had also been addressed. The restrictive Immigration Act of 1924 put severe limits on the number of southern Europeans, Eastern Europeans and East Asians who could legally immigrate to the United States. These immigration restrictions were trumpeted by Klan leaders and other anti-immigration groups, and this sense of a "solution" may have diminished the urgency associated with Klan recruiting.

Sociologist Rory McVeigh argued that the decline of the second phase of the Klan was in part an outcome of the group's initial successes. The 1924 election, argued McVeigh, demonstrated the political power wielded by the Klan, yet the Klan's trumpeting of its electoral power conversely meant that "members had to be convinced that their participation was still needed."[197] Klansmen, it seems, needed a sense of urgency to continue to remain dues-paying members, and the Ku Klux Klan simply failed to convey the atmosphere of impending crisis that it had been able to create in the past about supposed threats to "100 Percent Americanism."

Hiram Evans, imperial wizard of the Ku Klux Klan, celebrated the Klan's electoral successes in 1924 in an editorial in the Klan newspaper the *Kourier.*

No incident during 1924 so aptly displayed the solidarity of our organization and its influence for Americanism as did the elections in November. From Maine to California, from Kentucky to Minnesota, native-born Americans who have high standards of Americanism and personal rectitude of life were swept into office. Those who sought office through combinations of un-American influences were hopelessly defeated.[198]

The decline in the Ohio Klan additionally reflected local member discontent with expenditures by the state (Realm) officers of the organization. In its first few years of existence, the Ohio Realm collected as much as $10 million in dues from the local Klaverns with little in the way of charitable expenditures.[199] D.C. Stephenson claimed that in a two-year period he personally earned over $1.8 million as a Klan official, and Stephenson claimed that the national Klan offices raked in over $75 million in six years.[200] Salaries of Realm officers were rather excessive by employment standards at the time, and the Ohio Realm never got around to producing a balance sheet or accounting statements that were made available to representatives of local Klaverns.

Membership statewide in the Ohio Realm fell sharply in 1926 in figures supplied to a *New York Times* reporter by Grand Dragon Clyde W. Osborne. The state Klan officials reported 206,783 dues-paying members, and this figure included approximately 60,000 members of the women's auxiliary units.[201] Osborne, at the time, blamed the decline in membership on the elimination of "undesirable elements" from the ranks of local Klaverns, but the loss of approximately 100,000 members in less than three years cannot be solely blamed on local membership purges.

By 1928, the *New York Times* described the Ku Klux Klan in Ohio as being "almost negligible in politics." The newspaper noted that most Klan-supported candidates for political office were "badly beaten" since the impressive victories racked up by Klan-sponsored politicians in 1923 and 1924.[202] Yet local elections into the 1930s in Wood County featured candidates who were either Klan members at the time or who left the Klan in the period from 1928–31.

In Wood County, the 1924 election of the Reverend Rush A. Powell to the Ohio State Senate was a significant political victory for the Klan. However, the new job for Reverend Powell meant that he would be away in Columbus a great deal, and the minister's ability to work as a grass-roots organizer for the Klan was significantly reduced. Powell appears to have severed his association with the Klan by 1927, at least as a dues-paying member, and

The Knights of the KU KLUX KLAN

Are Continuing Their Fight

(Started 23 Years Ago)

For—	*Against—*
Christianity	Atheism
Individualism	Dictatorship
Liberty	Anarchy
Justice	Bolshevism
Education	Communism
Patriotism	*Fascism
Fraternity	*Naziism
Nationalism	Internationalism
Representative	and all other
Government	Anti-American "Isms"

*Fascism and Naziism are new names for the old world schemes to destroy
Liberty-Freedom-Individualism.

The KLAN *leads the way back to the Constitution and the* REPUBLIC *it Guarantees.*

JOIN NOW! The Ku Klux Klan Program is ACTION!

If interested, address, P. O. Box 1204, Atlanta, Ga.

KKK flyer, 1941. *Center for Archival Collections.*

the organizational responsibilities of his position as regional administrator for the United Brethren Church likely meant that he would have little time even if he wanted to continue promoting the Ku Klux Klan.

The effects of anti-Klan agitation cannot be overlooked in the decline of the Klan at the local level. In Wood County, several local newspapers kept up regular attacks on the Klan (most notably the *Wood County Democrat* and the *Daily Sentinel-Tribune*), and even the pro-Klan *Wood County Republican* began to limit coverage of the group's activities by the end of 1926.

Yet while the Klan in Wood County experienced significant membership losses beginning in 1926, the group did not fade as quickly as many other Klan chapters in the United States in the mid-1920s. Membership records show a faithful core of dozens of dues-paying members who continued to be active until the late 1930s.

In addition, numerous original members of the Wood County Klan joined a reformed Klan chapter that emerged in 1941. The group began collecting dues, organizing meetings and engaging in recruitment campaigns using some of the same tactics as used in the mid-1920s.

The Klan of the 1940s began to modify the tone of its messages to fit the changes brought about by the Second World War. The group identified Nazism and fascism as "Anti-American 'Isms'" that were "new names for the old world schemes to destroy Liberty-Freedom-Individualism." The Klan, according to the propaganda flyer, sought to lead the United States "back to the Constitution and the Republic it Guarantees."[203]

The reformed Wood County Klan held its meetings at 8:30 p.m. on Friday evenings at the Odd Fellows Hall in Portage. A complete list of officers for the 1940s-era Klan has survived, and all positions except the office of Kladd (the officer in charge of new member initiation) were filled.[204]

It is unclear exactly how many members joined the 1940s-era chapter of the Wood County Ku Klux Klan. At least nineteen individuals paid dues to the chapter in 1940 and 1941, and it is unknown if there were additional members of the chapter who had unofficial or non-dues-paying status.

The Ku Klux Klan maintained at least a nominal presence in Ohio during the era of the American civil rights movement. In one newspaper account, the grand dragon of the Ohio Ku Klux Klan renounced violence in a 1966 interview. Flynn Harvey of Columbus told an interviewer that if a Klan member engaged in violence, he would hope that "the law throws the book at him."[205] Yet despite the fact that Klan members staged several

A 1941 list of Klan officers. *Center for Archival Collections.*

cross burnings in Ohio in 1965 and representatives claimed chapters in five major Ohio cities, the FBI that year stated that Ohio was "not a state with significant Klan activity."[206]

A 1977 Klan rally at the Ohio state capitol building in Columbus turned violent. Imperial Wizard Dale R. Reusch of Lodi, Ohio, was attacked by anti-Klan protesters who ran past the fifty Columbus police officers assigned to protect the rallying Klansmen. Reusch suffered "facial lacerations, was stripped of his hooded purple uniform, spat at, hit by eggs, and thrown to the ground" by enraged protesters.[207]

There does not appear to have been a particularly active Klan chapter in Wood County in the decades after the Second World War. While the possibility remains that postwar Klan records may one day be discovered by researchers, an exploration of non-Klan sources in the period from 1945 to 1990 has not demonstrated any significant Wood County Klan activity during the era of the American civil rights movement and afterward. A representative of the Southern Poverty Law Center, which monitors hate groups, told the *Toledo Blade* in 1988 that the SPLC "did not have any documentation of an established Klan group" in the area. Racist incidents documented by the group at the time appear to have been "perpetrated by people who hold the same types of sentiments as members of white supremacist groups," said Pat Clark of the SPLC's Klanwatch project.[208]

The decade of the 1990s, however, would prove to be otherwise.

MILLENNIAL KLAN ACTIVITY IN WOOD COUNTY

Like many other areas of the country, Wood County experienced resurgence in Ku Klux Klan and other white supremacist activity toward the end of the twentieth century. While the number of dedicated white supremacists in the county is nowhere near the massive support the Klan received in the 1920s (and indeed is rather small by comparison), the county's legacy regarding white supremacist activity is slow to disappear.

In the 1990s, there was an increase in activity by Klan factions and other white supremacist groups. By the middle of the decade, nearly a dozen organized Klan groups were active in Ohio, according to Klanwatch, with perhaps as many as one thousand active Klan members in the state.

Part of the reason for the rise in the millennial resurgence of the Klan, Klan-affiliated groups and white supremacists is technological in nature. The emergence of the Internet has provided hate groups with an invaluable tool for recruitment of new members and the dissemination of information. The white supremacist movement had been relegated to the extreme margins of American society by the 1980s, but as the millennium approached, white supremacist and white nationalist groups appeared with greater frequency and activity in the United States.

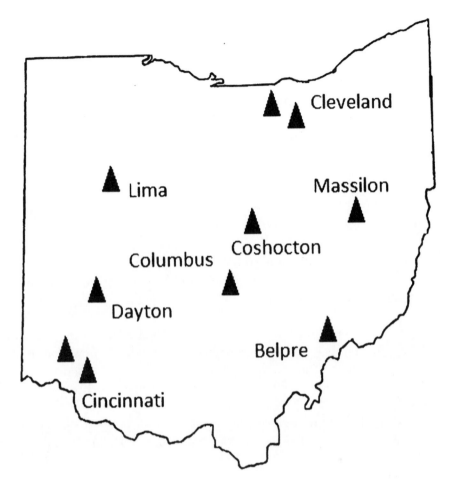

Map of known Klan chapters in Ohio, 1994. *Michael E. Brooks.*

The greater visibility of Klan and other white supremacist groups in the 1980s and 1990s also owed a debt to Klan operatives such as David Duke of Louisiana. The former grand wizard of the Klan became a media staple between 1975 and 1980, logging over one thousand appearances on television and radio programs in that time.[209] Duke later surprised political pundits by winning a seat in the U.S. Congress in 1989, and his campaigns for the U.S. Senate (1991) and the U.S. presidency (1992) provided a great deal of additional media exposure for the Ku Klux Klan.

THE 1994 KLAN RALLY IN BOWLING GREEN

Nine members of the Ohio Knights of the Ku Klux Klan—two of whom were young children—staged a rally in Bowling Green on June 18, 1994. The Klan event—part recruitment drive and part public spectacle—took place on the grounds of the Wood County courthouse. Approximately 250 people, mostly anti-Klan protesters, attended the event, which occurred the same day as another Klan rally in Toledo.

Ohio Klan grand titan Vincent J. Pinette told the crowd that he wanted "all white people to stand up and be proud of their heritage." Pinette said that he was "so tired of the Negroes saying that 'white man is oppressing me,'" claiming that "the Negro gets everything from the federal government: free medical benefits, free food stamps, free public housing." Pinette, taunting the crowd with racial stereotypes, argued that "in Africa, they'd still be living in shacks, and if they wanted to eat pork chops, they'd have to throw spears."[210]

Some violence occurred between participants at the 1994 Klan rally. The physical altercations that occurred at the 1994 Klan rally stemmed in part from the fact that police directed all attendees—pro-Klan and anti-Klan—into the same fenced-off area. A pro-Klan attendee from Sylvania, Ohio, had his Confederate flag T-shirt ripped off his body and torn to pieces.[211]

Several anti-Klan protesters were arrested by the police at the event. Marvetta Davis, a member of the National Women's Rights Organizing Coalition, was charged with a single count of inciting to violence.[212] Davis allegedly spit at a Klan supporter in the commotion. Others arrested as a result of the actions at the rally were identified from police photographs of people entering the security zone.[213]

Davis told reporters from the *Toledo Blade* that she was innocent of the charges brought against her. "It's sad that if you fight back against racism, you are the one that is prosecuted and not the people who are spouting the genocidal messages about killing blacks, Jews, gays, and lesbians."[214]

Wood County sheriff John Kohl noted that the event featured "loudness, spitting, ripping shirts off, slapping, pushing, and shoving." The sheriff also observed that "I had to bring horses in to get the people off the fence to keep them from trying to get the Klan."[215]

Approximately five hundred law enforcement officers were brought in to maintain order at the 1994 rally. Many of the officers traveled from nearby counties to assist in the event, and the Wood County sheriff engaged in reciprocal arrangements with other cities facing costly staffing for Klan rallies held that year.[216] City officials from Bowling Green and Toledo estimated that the cost of providing security for the two rallies exceeded $100,000.[217]

THE 1999 KLAN RALLY IN BOWLING GREEN

A different faction of the Ku Klux Klan petitioned to gather at the steps of the Wood County courthouse in 1999. The Knights of the White Kamellia notified Wood County that they wanted to stage a rally on July 19, 1999, to "inform the GOOD White people of Bowling Green that they still have a voice in America" and to "let people know that the Klan will always be here." The Klansman who wrote the letter, James Roesch of Bellefontaine, assured commissioners that the rally "will be a peaceful, non-violent assembly."[218]

Steve Kirk, grand dragon of the group, predicted that "25 to 60 Klan members" would travel to Bowling Green for the June 19 rally to hear the group's messages of "white pride, white rights, [and] white unity." Kirk, in an interview before the rally with the *Sentinel-Tribune*, said that his group was particularly concerned with "race mixing," which extended beyond interracial dating to include any interaction between people of different races.[219]

Kirk claimed that there already existed members of his Klan faction active in Wood County. The Klan leader, however, refused to divulge names of Klan members or to provide an estimate of the number of Klan members in his group who were Wood County residents.[220]

Unlike the 1994 Klan rally in Bowling Green, attendees of the Klan rally in 1999 were separated into one of two "fenced-in spectator areas" in the 200 block of East Court Street near the courthouse. Sheriff John Kohl indicated that the decision to separate pro-Klan and anti-Klan spectators was a "safety-driven measure intended to reduce the threat of violence" between the two groups.[221]

Kirk's predictions of a large turnout by his Klan faction appear to have been overly optimistic. The *Toledo Blade* and the *Daily Sentinel-Tribune* reported that only twelve members of the Knights of the White Kamellia showed up for the Saturday rally, while only one pro-Klan supporter entered the Klan spectator area. Defiance County sheriff Dave Westrick, on hand to help secure the rally site, described the Klan rally as "pathetic."[222] There were no injuries or arrests at this public Klan event.

The cost of providing security for the 1999 Klan rally in Bowling Green was estimated to be as much as $25,000. Costs included overtime payments to Bowling Green police and Wood County deputy sheriffs, the rental of chain-link security fencing, special uniforms and food for the officers on duty.[223]

In both the 1994 and 1999 Klan rallies, an alternate form of local anti-Klan resistance emerged. For both rallies, a group known as the Unity Day Coalition formed to "reclaim our community from the hatred brought to our town by the KKK rally."[224] The coalition urged residents to ignore the rally and engage in positive, family-oriented activities such as visits to the park or zoo, going bowling, visiting the art museum or cleaning out the garage.[225] For each rally, the Unity Day Coalition held a candlelight vigil the night before and then led a "reclamation" ceremony the day after.[226]

The coalition's efforts may indeed have paid off in 1999. Attendance at the 1999 Klan rally was much lower, and the near absence of violence perhaps attests to the power of a unified, nonviolent opposition to the views of the Ku Klux Klan.

POST-2000 KLAN ACTIVITY IN WOOD COUNTY

Ohio continues to remain a state with active Ku Klux Klan and white supremacist groups. The state is noted for the organization known as the Brotherhood of Ku Klux Klans (BOK), which is headquartered in Marion, Ohio. The group was the second-largest Klan organization in the United States, with thirty-eight chapters as recently as 2010, though the defection of a major Klan leader to the neo-Nazi Aryan Nations likely has reduced the power of the BOK.[227]

Organized activity by the Ku Klux Klan and affiliated white supremacist groups in Wood County, though, has been comparatively quiet in the years since the start of the new millennium. Several Wood County residents participated in the white supremacist rallies organized in Toledo, Ohio, by the neo-Nazi National Socialist Movement (NSM) in October and December 2005, but the anti-racist group Southern Poverty Law Center is currently monitoring only one hate group in Wood County (a Christian Identity operation in Fostoria, Ohio).[228]

While organized Klan and white supremacist activity in Wood County has dwindled in comparison with the Ku Klux Klan of the 1920s, it would be overly optimistic to make the claim that the county is free from racism and other forms of intolerance. There have been a number of racist incidents in the county in the past several years, and residents in the county continue to grapple with issues related to bigotry and religious intolerance.

In September 2012, an arsonist set fire to a golden-domed mosque known as the Islamic Center of Greater Toledo, which is located in Perrysburg. The blaze caused significant water and smoke damage throughout the facility, forcing extensive renovations to the mosque.[229] Police later arrested Randolph Linn of St. Joe, Indiana, in the crime, and after pleading guilty, Linn received a sentence of twenty years in prison.[230]

In October 2012, a group of teenagers in Bowling Green drew swastikas and the words "White Power" on the driveway and sidewalk of an African American family.[231] The teenagers happened to select the home of Louis Orr, the men's basketball coach at Bowling Green State University, a fact that brought significant national media attention to the event.

The day after the incident involving the home of Louis Orr, the automobile of another African American resident of Bowling Green was targeted in an apparent act of racism. A twenty-four-year-old BGSU student named Chad Franklin found watermelons smashed on his vehicle along with a "racially charged" note.[232]

White patrons of a Bowling Green nightclub apparently became upset after a group of African Americans entered the facility in April 2013. Several people accessed the social media platform Twitter and issued inflammatory tweets, labeling the African Americans as a "chocolate ocean" and using overtly racist language to describe the black patrons.[233]

In response to the recent series of racist incidents, the city of Bowling Green and Bowling Green State University joined a national initiative known as "Not in Our Town." The goals of the campaign are to "to affirm their commitment to social justice, equity and inclusion as well as embrace and celebrate diversity."[234] Perhaps the "Not in Our Town" campaign and other related efforts will further reduce the likelihood that the Ku Klux Klan will ever reemerge in Wood County as a disruptive force in the community.

GLOSSARY OF KLAN TERMINOLOGY

AKIA: acronymic greeting meaning "A Klansman I Am."

alien: anyone who is not a Klan member.

banish: to force out a Klan member from a Klavern.

domains: groups of states in the Invisible Empire (same boundaries as U.S. states).

Empire Mutual: corporation created to sell life insurance to Klan members.

exalted cyclops: president of a Klavern.

grand dragon: leader of Klan realm.

grand giant: honorary term for a former grand dragon.

grand goblin: sales manager of Klan memberships for a particular domain.

hydras: generic term used for officers of a particular Realm.

Imperial Kloncilium: advisory board for the national Klan, also known as "Genii."

imperial tax: portion of local dues sent to national headquarters.

imperial wizard: national leader of the Ku Klux Klan (also known as "grand wizard").

Glossary of Klan Terminology

Inner Circle: select group of Klan leaders responsible for planning covert action.

ITSUB: Klan sign-off in correspondence meaning "In the Sacred Unfailing Bond."

Junior Order: youth auxiliary KKK unit.

kalendar: dating system used by the KKK beginning with the rebirth year of 1915.

king kleagle: officer responsible for establishing new chapters at regional levels.

klabee: treasurer of a local chapter.

kladd: official responsible for initiating new members in a local chapter.

klaliff: vice-president of a local chapter.

Klanishness: behaviors and rituals expected of Klan members (sometimes known as Klankraft); often used to describe economic activity by Klan members, such as buying only from known Klan members and avoiding purchases from non-Klan businesses.

Klansman: a member of the Ku Klux Klan.

klanton: area of jurisdiction for a local Klan chapter.

klarogo: sergeant-at-arms of a local chapter.

klavalier: military detachment of the Klan used primarily as protection during meetings.

klavern: a local chapter of the Ku Klux Klan.

klazik: second vice-president at Imperial level.

kleagle: Klan officer responsible for recruiting new members at the local level.

klectoken: initiation fee.

klepeer: a delegate sent to the Imperial Klonvokation.

kligrapp: secretary of a local chapter.

klokard: lecturer of a local chapter.

Klonklave: regional meeting of Klan chapters (also spelled "Konklave").

GLOSSARY OF KLAN TERMINOLOGY

klonversation: the use of Klan passwords and code words between Klan members.

klonverse: meeting between Klan members at the provincial level.

Klonvokation: national convention of the Klan (also spelled "Klanvocation").

Kloran: handbook of Klan rituals.

Klorero: state convention with representatives from local Klan chapters.

kludd: chaplain of a local chapter.

Kluxer: member of a Klan chapter.

Kluxing: the act of promoting the Klan.

knight: first-degree member of KKK.

knight kamelia: second-degree member of KKK (also known as K-Duo).

knight of the great forest: third-degree member of KKK (also known as K-Trio).

knight of the midnight mystery: fourth-degree member of KKK (also known as K-Quad).

naturalization: the initiation ceremony of the Klan.

nighthawk: courier of a local chapter.

non silba sed anthar: Latin phrase used by Klans meaning "Not for one's self, but for others."

province: regional subdivisions within individual states.

Realm: individual state within the Invisible Empire (same boundaries as U.S. states).

Realm tax: portion of local dues sent to state headquarters.

SANBOG: acronym meaning "Strangers Are Near, Be On Guard."

terrors: generic term for the officers of a Klavern.

Women of the Ku Klux Klan: women's auxiliary KKK units.

Appendix I

MEMBERS OF THE WOOD COUNTY KLAVERN OF THE KU KLUX KLAN, 1923-41

A

Abraham, Leedy Cocanour
(Perrysburg)
Adams, Harley A. (North Baltimore)
Adams, Harrison Canright (Bowling
Green)
Adkins, Fred M. (Bradner)
Agen, John H. (Mermill)
Aiken, Jay A. (North Baltimore)
Aldridge, Frank H. (Mermill)
Allen, John J. (Bowling Green)
Amerine, John (Colton)
Amos, Clarence J. (Portage)
Anderson, C.C. (Bowling Green)
Angel, Jay Leonard (Bowling Green)
Anspach, George F. (North Baltimore)
Anspach, G.F. (North Baltimore)
Anthony, Lester (Cygnet)
Apple, James Henry (North Baltimore)
Archer, James Marion (North
Baltimore)
Archibold, Thomas (Prairie Depot)
Arnold, Ray Vance (Bowling Green)
Artz, Elbert Howard (Maumee)
Asmus, Edward "Ted" Walter (Bowling
Green)
Atwell, Harvey E. (Bowling Green)

Austin, George Lewis (Bowling Green)
Austin, Percy Leroy (Haskins)
Austin, Robert Werlyn (Bowling Green)
Avery, Bernard Heminger (Bowling
Green)
Avery, Ray Dudley (Bowling Green)
Avey, Leonard H. (Cygnet)

B

Babcock, Joseph S. (Bowling Green)
Backman, Ira William (Grand Rapids)
Badders, Elmer J. (Bowling Green)
Baightel, George Dewitt (Grand
Rapids)
Bailey, Earl E. (Bowling Green)
Bain, Frank H. (Bowling Green)
Baker, Bernard J. (Walbridge)
Baker, Charles E. (Prairie Depot)
Baker, David J. (North Baltimore)
Baker, Leander A. (Bairdstown)
Baker, Zera (Risingsun)
Baldwin, Dewey (Bowling Green)
Baltz, Earl S. (North Baltimore)
Baltz, Harry Clyde (Cygnet)
Baltz, William M. (North Baltimore)
Banister, William M. (Weston)
Banks, William S. (Scotch Ridge)

Barber, George Allen (Weston)
Bard, Ora "Orrie" W. (Cygnet)
Barhite, John (Tontogany)
Barringer, Carl C. (Bairdstown)
Barritt, Earl S.(Bowling Green)
Barron, John M. (Bowling Green)
Basom, Russell M. (Portage)
Bates, Edward R. (Bowling Green)
Bates, Harold R. (Bowling Green)
Bates, Russell Albert (Bowling Green)
Batey, Archie (Prairie Depot)
Bauman, Leonard (Toledo)
Bear, Eastman M. (Perrysburg)
Beard, Earl E. (Portage)
Beard, James M. (Portage)
Beaverson, Ellsworth J. (Dowling)
Beaverson, Fred (Tontogany)
Beckman, Norman George (Haskins)
Beddoe, William John (Perrysburg)
Belleville, Loy E. (Bowling Green)
Bema, Edgar S. (Dunbridge)
Bemis, Charles J. (Haskins)
Bemis, Fred E. (Haskins)
Bemis, Gordon Ralph (Haskins)
Bennett, Leroy H. (Toledo)
Bernard, Henry (North Baltimore)
Berndt, Rolland F. (Bowling Green)
Bevard, Wayne Everett (Walbridge)
Bevelhymer, John A. (Bowling Green)
Biebesheimer, William J. (Perrysburg)
Bigelow, Ralph Lee (Rudolph)
Bistline, Barney O. (Bowling Green)
Bittle, George L. (Bowling Green)
Bittle, Robert M. (Bowling Green)
Black, George W. (North Baltimore)
Blackburn, William (Milton Center)
Blake, James Seneca (North Baltimore)
Bland, Grover Eugene (North Baltimore)
Blasius Henry (Custar)
Blasius, Lloyd Wesley (Custar)
Blasius, Matthias P. (Custar)
Bloom, David L. (North Baltimore)
Bobb, John A. (North Baltimore)
Boggs, Elza (Rudolph)

Boggs, Fred A. (Rudolph)
Bomer, Ira E. (North Baltimore)
Bonner, Elmer J. (North Baltimore)
Bonner, Guy (North Baltimore)
Book, Harry M. (Bowling Green)
Boosenbark, William M. (Bowling Green)
Bordner, George (Weston)
Bosler, Augustus "Gus" Howard (North Baltimore)
Bosler, True L. (North Baltimore)
Bostick, Landon A. (Bowling Green)
Bostick, Otto Thomas (Bowling Green)
Bourquin, Donnan L. (Bowling Green)
Bowen, Bert (Bowling Green)
Bowers, Charles R. (Grand Rapids)
Bowers, Elmer James (Bowling Green)
Bowers, Flora William (Prairie Depot)
Bowers, John P. (Prairie Depot)
Bowers, Louis E. (Bradner)
Bowers, Ray E. (Bowling Green)
Bowman, Leslie H. (Rossford)
Bowman, William C. (Cygnet)
Box, Russell Claire (Grand Rapids)
Boyd, Henry D. (Fostoria)
Boyles, Elmer Larue (Bowling Green)
Braka, Orson (Perrysburg)
Bray, John W. (Bowling Green)
Bressler, Brice H. (Bowling Green)
Bressler, John Freeland (Bloomdale)
Bressler, Merton C. (Bowling Green)
Briggs, A.L. (Bowling Green)
Brigham, Haven A. (Bowling Green)
Brigham, Joel Winfield (Bowling Green)
Brim, David Raymond (Portage)
Brink, George Alva (Rudolph)
Brink, Lester Eugene (Rudolph)
Broka, Rutherford Warren (Sugar Ridge)
Brooks, Oakley John (Bowling Green)
Brossia, Albert Philip (Perrysburg)
Brossia, Edward Charles (Perrysburg)
Brough, Holl M. (Genoa)
Brown, Arthur R. (Custar)
Brown, Clarence (North Baltimore)

Brown, Clarence H. (Prairie Depot)
Brown, Harry M. (Rossford)
Browne, William Manville (Bowling Green)
Brownweller, M.J. (Milton Center)
Broyles, Louis A. (Prairie Depot)
Brubaker, Clyde C. (Rossford)
Bruce, Lewis Lawrence (Dunbridge)
Brush, Elvis [Elvie] D. (Maumee)
Bryant, A.W. (Bloomdale)
Buchanan, Curtis Nathaniel (North Baltimore)
Burditt, Arthur (Weston)
Burditt, Clarence R. (Tontogany)
Burgermeister, Reuben W. (Perrysburg)
Burkhalter, Harry D. (Bowling Green)
Burns, Virgil N. (Prairie Depot)
Burris, Charles Elmer (Bairdstown)
Burris, J.H. (Bairdstown)
Bursick, Edward J. (Jerry City)
Bursick, William Henry (Jerry City)
Burson, Leon G. (Custar)
Burton, Floyd A. (Bowling Green)
Bushey, David B. (North Baltimore)
Butler, Ernest Melville (Bowling Green)
Butturff, Charles D. (Bowling Green)
Byham, Allen S. (Rudolph)
Byrne, F.A. (Prairie Depot)

C

Cable, James Robinson (Walbridge)
Cable, Henry (Walbridge)
Caldwell, George Raymond (Portage)
Campbell, Charles R. (North Baltimore)
Campbell, Harry C. (Bowling Green)
Campbell, Henry E. (Bowling Green)
Campbell, Paul (Bowling Green)
Campbell, William H. (Milton Center)
Campbell, Wilson V. (Bowling Green)
Canfield, Dwight Reuben (Perrysburg)
Cannon, Robert L. (Toledo)
Carnicom, Harry F. (Rudolph)
Carnicom, John Wesley (Bowling Green)

Carnicom, William L. (Rudolph)
Carpenter, Carey Lloyd (Haskins)
Carpenter, Philip B. (Prairie Depot)
Carpenter, William H. (Bowling Green)
Carr, Arthur Edmond (Cygnet)
Carr, Arthur J. (Bowling Green)
Carr, John E. (Cygnet)
Carr, Robert D. (Rossford)
Carston, Hollis Oratio (Prairie Depot)
Carter, Earnest W. (Perrysburg)
Carter, Isaac N. (Bowling Green)
Carter, Ray C. (Toledo)
Carter, Ray R. (Perrysburg)
Castle, William T. (North Baltimore)
Caswell, Walter Duel (Custar)
Caza, James Noel (Rossford)
Challen, Edgar R. (Custar)
Chamberlain, Donald P. (Bowling Green)
Chamberlain, Francis A. (Prairie Depot)
Chamberlain, James E. (Bowling Green)
Chamberlain, Kenneth A. (Mermill)
Chamberlain, Lewis (Bowling Green)
Chamberlain, Sherman (Bowling Green)
Chamberlain, Theron (Bowling Green)
Chamberlain, Zenas R. (Perrysburg)
Chamberlin, Royal Francis (Bowling Green)
Champion, Frank (Tontogany)
Chapman, George B. (Bowling Green)
Charles, William W., Jr. (Perrysburg)
Chilcote, Cyril Y. (Bowling Green)
Chilcote, Leander "Lee" J. (West Milgrove)
Chittenden, George A. (Bowling Green)
Christiansen, Martin (Walbridge)
Christiansen, Merle (Walbridge)
Clark, Albert C. (Rossford)
Clark, Frank (Bowling Green)
Clark, Levi Herman (Mermill)
Clarke, Frederick Z., Jr. (Rossford)
Clements, Clifford Lloyd (Portage)

Clouser, George Alvin (North Baltimore)
Clouser, Harry Aloys (North Baltimore)
Clouser, William B. (North Baltimore)
Cluxton, Clarence Irwin (Portage)
Cobb, Earl H. (Portage)
Coen, Arley E. (Bowling Green)
Coen, Frank M. (Bowling Green)
Coen, Gerald H. (Bowling Green)
Coen, Harold M. (Bowling Green)
Coen, Layton E. (Bowling Green)
Coger, Alva (Cygnet)
Coger, Claude M. (Cygnet)
Coger, Clinton C. (Cygnet)
Coger, Dewey D. (Cygnet)
Coger, William C. (Mermill)
Cole, Charles J. (Custar)
Cole, Lester J. (Bowling Green)
Cole, Marvin D. (Rossford)
Collins, Alfred Jacob (Bowling Green)
Collins, George (Sugar Ridge)
Compton, Ruben Strait (Perrysburg)
Conklin, James M. (Weston)
Conley, Asa Ross (Pemberville)
Conner, Elmer M. (Rossford)
Conner, John M. (Rossford)
Conrad, William Orval (North Baltimore)
Cook, Archie Kennedy (Bowling Green)
Cook, Frederick R. (Bowling Green)
Cook, Silas E. (Risingsun)
Cook, Warren V. (Toledo)
Cookson, William Albert (Bowling Green)
Cooper, Lewis W. (Bowling Green)
Cope, William Floyd (Perrysburg)
Copus, Edwin C. (Bowling Green)
Corbett, John C. (Rudolph)
Cordrey, James Frank (Dowling)
Cordrey, Marion Lloyd (Bowling Green)
Cordrey, Milan (Bowling Green)
Cox, Charles M. (Rudolph)
Crandall, Leon William (Perrysburg)
Craven, Earnest M. (Perrysburg)

Crawford, Homer E. (Bowling Green)
Crepps, Harry Lynn (Custar)
Crepps, John L. (Custar)
Creps, Addison Dallas (North Baltimore)
Crom, Carlton W. (Bowling Green)
Crom, John Alanson (Clyde)
Cron, Howard (Bowling Green)
Cron, Irvin (Bowling Green)
Cron, Roscoe H. (Bowling Green)
Cross, Henry E. (Bowling Green)
Crouse, Leo Idell (North Baltimore)
Cummins, Thomas O. (Perrysburg)
Cunning, Hiram J. (Haskins)
Cupp, John W. (North Baltimore)
Cupp, Thomas J. (Bowling Green)
Curlis, Thomas M. (Bowling Green)
Current, Alvin Charles (Tontogany)
Current, Charles Elford (Dunbridge)
Curry, Jesse J. (Bowling Green)
Curry, Samuel H. (Bradner)
Curtis, Lewis William (Rudolph)

D

Dailey, Dwight E. (North Baltimore)
Damon, Cloyce Cecil (North Baltimore)
Danford, Edward I., Jr. (Rossford)
Danford, Edward I., Sr. (Rossford)
Dauterman, Andrew J. (Portage)
Dauterman, Clifton Roy (Portage)
Davenport, Clesson M. (Rossford)
Davenport, H. (Perrysburg)
Davenport, John M. (Dowling)
Davenport, Ray W. (Bowling Green)
Davenport, Rex (Toledo)
Davis, Edward C. (Bowling Green)
Davis, Edward G. (Weston)
Davis, Jay N. (North Baltimore)
Davis, O.T. (Perrysburg)
Davis, Walter L. (Portage)
Day, Ezra F. (Prairie Depot)
Day, Louis J (Bairdstown)
Deck, John Franklin (Bowling Green)
DeLaney, Bruce S. (Cygnet)
DeLong, Howard Joseph (Weston)

Denhoff, Harold J. (Prairie Depot)
Denman, William H. (Bowling Green)
Dennis, Alfred V. (Bowling Green)
Dennis, Alvin Charles (Dunbridge)
Dennis, Bert Lee (Dowling)
Dennis, Dean I. (Bowling Green)
Dennis, Earl Marion (Dunbridge)
Dennis, Fred Otto (Bowling Green)
Dennis, Freed [Fred] (Bloomdale)
Dennis, M.S. (Bloomdale)
Dennis, Vivian H. (Dowling)
Dennis, Willard (Dunbridge)
DeRodes, Harry Cecil (North Baltimore)
Deter, Carl E. (North Baltimore)
Deter, John William (North Baltimore)
Deutschman, Alfred L. (Bowling Green)
Deverna, Dwight Harold (Perrysburg)
DeWitt, Fred (Bowling Green)
Dewyer, Milo (Bloomdale)
Dick, Earl E. (North Baltimore)
Dicken, Charles Frank (Prairie Depot)
Dicken, Curtis (Prairie Depot)
Dickey, Charles F. (Weston)
Dieter, Jacob H. (Prairie Depot)
Dieter, John H. (Prairie Depot)
Digby, Bert E. (Grand Rapids)
Digby, Lloyd (Bowling Green)
Digby, Roy E. (Bowling Green)
Dill, Lester H. (Custar)
Dillinger, Herbert "Herby" Harland (Hoytville)
Dimick, Leland Marshall (Bowling Green)
Dimick, Marshall Chester (Perrysburg)
Dipman, Warren Oscar (Toledo)
Dishong, Floyd M. (Deshler)
Dodge, Julius (Perrysburg)
Doering, Charles Mitchell (Bairdstown)
Doering, Howard O., Sr. (Bairdstown)
Donahey, William C. (Bowling Green)
Doty, Everett A. (Cygnet)
Doughty, Denver D. (Walbridge)
Down, Clarence D. (Bowling Green)

Downs, Bert "Bud" Harrison (North Baltimore)
Downs, Clarence B. (Bowling Green)
Downs, Samuel Clinton (North Baltimore)
Downs, Samuel Clinton (Rossford)
Drain, Eldon Nicholas (Portage)
Drake, Jay Jonas (Pemberville)
Drake, Ralph Lowe (Pemberville)
Drew, Roscoe G. (Bloomdale)
Ducat, Earl D. (Walbridge)
Ducat, Lloyd J. (Bowling Green)
Duesler, Harry C. (Rudolph)
Duesler, Miles U. (Jerry City)
Duesler, Preston Harry (Rudolph)
Dukes, Carl (North Baltimore)
Dulaney, Elijah A. (North Baltimore)
Dulaney, William W. (North Baltimore)
Duquett, Ralph Waldo (Bradner)
Duquett, William J. (Bradner)
Dyer, Luther O. (Prairie Depot)
Dyer, Seymour F. (Prairie Depot)
Dysinger, Howard L. (North Baltimore)

E

Earleywine, George W. (North Baltimore)
Eberly, Roy B. (Bowling Green)
Eckert, Bert Ray (Rudolph)
Eckert, E.J. (North Baltimore)
Eckert, John M. (Mermill)
Eckert, Rolland "Rollie" W. (Portage)
Edwards, Elmer (Weston)
Edwards, Ray O. (Rudolph)
Edwards, Vernon R. (Toledo)
Eiben, Joseph C. (North Baltimore)
Elarton, Duane Merlon (Prairie Depot)
Elarton, Floren Dow (Prairie Depot)
Elarton, Lloyd D. (Rossford)
Ellerman, Edward John (Lime City)
Ellsworth, Albert L. (Bowling Green)
Ellsworth, Cecil Butruff (Bowling Green)
Elsea, Guy Newton (Bowling Green)

Elwing, Walter F. (Rossford)
Emahiser, Clifton B. (Risingsun)
Emahiser, Roscoe, Elden (Risingsun)
Emch, Carl William (Pemberville)
Emery, S.B. (Haskins)
Emmerich, Homer Harvey (Bowling Green)
England, Charles Wesley (Bowling Green)
England, George W. (Dowling)
England, Howard R. (Bowling Green)
Engle, Ralph P. (Bowling Green)
Englehart, Calvin B. (Luckey)
English, Roscoe "Ross" Jesse (Bowling Green)
English, Virgil R. (Bowling Green)
English, Wendell (Bowling Green)
Errett, Daniel W. (Bowling Green)
Errett, David "Frank" Franklin (Weston)
Errett, William, Jerry (Bowling Green)
Ershick, Alanzo (Bowling Green)
Essex, Orion F. (Bradner)
Euler, Cecil (Bowling Green)
Evans, Dale (Prairie Depot)
Evans, L.K. (Rudolph)
Evans, McClelland (Portage)
Evans, Robert A. (Rudolph)
Evans, William E. (Portage)
Evers, Jessie M. (Prairie Depot)

F

Farrison, Blair Albert (McClure)
Fellers, Forrest Stanley (Bowling Green)
Fellers, Jacob Tilden (North Baltimore)
Fellers, Oliver Albert (North Baltimore)
Feltman, George (Prairie Depot)
Ferguson, John Allen (Weston)
Fetterman, Cyrus E. (Portage)
Finch, Forest R. (Bowling Green)
Finch, Ira Franklin (Perrysburg)
Finch, Theodore (Rossford)
Finch, William Mac (Perrysburg)
Findley, Harvey Harrison (Cygnet)

Finkenbiner, Trivet Sylvester (Bowling Green)
Finney, Odd (Bowling Green)
Fish, Edward (Weston)
Fish, Eldon W. (Bowling Green)
Fisher, Emerson Webster (Portage)
Fisher, L.H. (Bowling Green)
Fletcher, Charles E. (Bowling Green)
Flower, Guy William (Rudolph)
Fogle, Philip Augustine (Rudolph)
Fogler, Sheridan "Sherd" (Rudolph)
Foor, John C. (Pemberville)
Foot, M.L. (Grand Rapids)
Ford, George H. (Rudolph)
Ford, George W. (Rudolph)
Ford, Glenn G. (Rudolph)
Forrester, Walter (Bowling Green)
Foster, John H. (Portage)
Fox, Elmer L. (Perrysburg)
Fox, Frank E (Perrysburg)
Frampton, Claud B. (Cygnet)
Francisco, Byron S. (North Baltimore)
Frank, Kenneth Homer (Rudolph)
Frantz, Earl (Rossford)
Frantz, Sam (Bowling Green)
Frantz, Samuel H. (Rossford)
Frederick, Edward M. (North Baltimore)
Frederick, Ernest Allen (North Baltimore)
Fredrick, J.F. (Bowling Green)
Fredrick, Orestus J. (Rossford)
Fredericks, Virgil (Vergie) Blake (Bowling Green)
Freeman, W.E. (Rossford)
Freyman, Irvin (Irven) Illion (Portage)
Freyman, Perry Emmitt (Bowling Green)
Frick, George C. (Rossford)
Friess, Robert Amos (Perrysburg)
Frolrise, John (Perrysburg)
Fry, William H. (Bowling Green)
Fryman, Earl Thomas (Portage)
Fuller, Calvin "Hub" H. (Perrysburg)
Fuller, Orville Clifford (Bowling Green)

G

Gallier, Dale W. (Bowling Green)
Gallier, Everett Paul (Bowling Green)
Gallier, Horace Arthur (Bowling Green)
Gallier, James G. (Bowling Green)
Gamble, Glenn C. (Rudolph)
Gander, Bliss Pangle (Bowling Green)
Garberson, Harvey Alfred (Walbridge)
Garrison, Lewis L. (North Baltimore)
Garrison, Samuel Hass (North Baltimore)
Gebert, Howard Leston (Bowling Green)
Gehring, A.J. (Bowling Green)
Genson, Richard Silas (Haskins)
George, Roscoe F. (Bowling Green)
George, Victor Dewey (Bowling Green)
Gernert, William Henry (Bowling Green)
Gibben, J.N. (Bowling Green)
Gibson, Arthur J. (Bowling Green)
Gilbert, Fenton G. (Walbridge)
Gilham, John F. (Pemberville)
Gill, Frederick (Grand Rapids)
Gillian, Carmel (Portage)
Ginder, David Oliver (Bowling Green)
Glaser, Clarence J. (Bowling Green)
Glaser, Cyrus (Cirus) E. (Mermill)
Glassford, Albert Winfield (North Baltimore)
Glassford, James W. (Rudolph)
Goforth, John C. (Rossford)
Gokey, Clarence W. (Bowling Green)
Gokey, William (Bowling Green)
Gonyer, Henry (Bowling Green)
Gooch, Luther Bundy (Prairie Depot)
Good, Carl M., Sr., Bloomdale)
Good, John W. (Prairie Depot)
Goodell, Cyrenius E. (Luckey)
Goodell, Myrt Darwin (Luckey)
Goodell, Sanford E. (Luckey)
Goodman, Bert Leroy (Bowling Green)
Goodman, Charles H. (Bowling Green)
Goodman, Chauncey Clement (Perrysburg)
Goodman, Jesse D. (Bowling Green)
Graber, Adam J. (Prairie Depot)
Graf, Emil D. (McClure)
Graham, Lee Roy (Bloomdale)
Grames, George W. (Tontogany)
Grant, George E., Jr. (Cygnet)
Grant, George E., Sr. (Cygnet)
Gray, Benjamin B. (Columbus)
Greeley, Ashford H. (Bowling Green)
Greeley, Sidney (Weston)
Green, Herman W. (Bowling Green)
Green, Richard H. (Bowling Green)
Greenfield, Lewis Webster (Weston)
Greer, Archie Otho (Bowling Green)
Griffith, John W. (Bowling Green)
Griffith, William J.S. (Bowling Green)
Grover, Orlando Douglass (Sugar Ridge)
Gustin, Forest F. (Bowling Green)
Gustin, Howard F. (Bowling Green)

H

Haas, Julius I. (Custar)
Haefner, Fredrick W. (Perrysburg)
Haefner, Harvey B. (Perrysburg)
Haefner [Hafner] Vincent J. (Perrysburg)
Hahn, Charles George (Perrysburg)
Hainer, Charles Ogle (Cygnet)
Haines, Eldridge R. (Bowling Green)
Halbert, Miles G. (Haskins)
Hale, Arthur Gregory (Dunbridge)
Hale, Fred E. (Bowling Green)
Hall, Fred Jerome (Haskins)
Hall, Price A. (Toledo)
Halliman, William (Bowling Green)
Hamilton, Fred (Prairie Depot)
Hamman, Perry E. (Cygnet)
Hammond, McRoy "Roy" A. (Cygnet)
Hanawalt, Arthur (Bowling Green)
Hankey, Don Brown (Bowling Green)
Hanley, Clarence H. (Lemoyne)
Hanselman, Louis M. (Rossford)
Hansen, Ira Paul (Walbridge)
Hanson, Frederick K. (Perrysburg)

Harbour, Ellsworth Clare (Perrysburg)
Harker, Edward Percival (Rossford)
Harkness, Charles S. (Cygnet)
Harlow, Donald J. (Bowling Green)
Harman, Frank D. (Prairie Depot)
Harman, George F. (Prairie Depot)
Harman, Harry Ray (Bowling Green)
Harman, John (Prairie Depot)
Harman, Nelson Elwood (Prairie Depot)
Harper, Harvey B. (Weston)
Harper, Herman H. (Perrysburg)
Harris, Frank Benjamin (Rudolph)
Harris, Oliver A. (Van Buren)
Harris, William A. (Bowling Green)
Harrison, Thomas (Portage)
Hartzog, Arley Rochelle (Bowling Green)
Hatfield, Charles Bonnell (Bloomdale)
Hatfield, Harvy (Portage)
Hatfield, Leonard Samuel (Portage)
Hatfield, Ralph D (Bloomdale)
Hathaway, John W. (Milton Center)
Hauck, Charles J. (North Baltimore)
Hawks, Morris C. (Maumee)
Hayner, Clyde (Portage)
Hazelton, Chester Dale (North Baltimore)
Hazelwood, M.C. (Tontogany)
Hazelwood, William C. (Tontogany)
Healey, Sidney (Walbridge)
Healey, William B. (Walbridge)
Heath, Clarence Burdell (Portage)
Heckart, Charles "Charley" C. (Luckey)
Heckart, Frank Elmer (Luckey)
Heckman, John E. (Bowling Green)
Heilman, Harold Henry (Hoytville)
Heineman, Henry H. (Rossford)
Helzer, Leroy "Roy" Lee (Luckey)
Hemelspeck, Edward J. (Tontogany)
Heminger, Irvin Orville (North Baltimore)
Hemminger, James R. (Weston)
Hemminger, Olan S. (Tontogany)
Hemminger, Samuel (Tontogany)

Hempey, Olester Guy (Bowling Green)
Henderson, Dick (Rossford)
Henderson, George Albert (Rossford)
Henderson, James H. (Prairie Depot)
Henderson, Lawrence C. (Mermill)
Henderson, Robert F. (Weston)
Hendricks, Dewey (Bowling Green)
Hendricks, John D (Bowling Green)
Hengsteller, Samuel B (Prairie Depot)
Henline, Dale W. (Bloomdale)
Herbert, Archie (Bowling Green)
Herbert, Evan H. (Bowling Green)
Herringshair, Fred M. (Custar)
Herringshair, W.F. (Custar)
Herringshaw, Harold C. (Custar)
Herringshaw, Thomas (Bowling Green)
Hess, William R. (North Baltimore)
Hesse, William H. (Bowling Green)
Heubner, Henry W. (Tontogany)
Heyman, Alvy (Grand Rapids)
Hight, John P. (Risingsun)
Higley, Jess P. (Risingsun)
Hill, Irvin J. (Prairie Depot)
Hill, Lester D. (Bowling Green)
Hill, Levi Harrison (Rossford)
Hilliard, Charles R. (Rudolph)
Himes, Arthur Q. (Portage)
Himes, Charles E. (Rudolph)
Himes, Friend Robert (Portage)
Hiser, C.M. (Bradner)
Hite, James A. (Bowling Green)
Hite, Orla [Orly] D. (Bowling Green)
Hoaglin, Nicholas (Cygnet)
Hockett, Stephen Otto (Perrysburg)
Hodgeman, Stanley F. (Weston)
Hoffkins, Ernest Winfred (Bowling Green)
Holeman, Perry Elmer (Cygnet)
Holenbaugh, Jerome (Cass Township)
Holloway, Henry H. (Bowling Green)
Hommes, George (Perrysburg)
Hoobler, Asher Lafayette (North Baltimore)
Hoover, Arthur Deroy (Cygnet)

136

Hopkins, Edward Stanton (Bowling Green)
Hopper, George O. (Bowling Green)
Hoskinson, Jacob C. (Rudolph)
Hoskinson, Levi R. (Bowling Green)
Hostetter, Victor Grant (Bowling Green)
Hottman, Carl G. (Bowling Green)
Householder, Everrett Earnest (Bowling Green)
Householder, Solomon Reverda (Bowling Green)
Hudson, Kenneth S. (Bowling Green)
Huffman, Maurice John (North Baltimore)
Hufford, Alfred C. (Perrysburg)
Hughes, Frank J. (Bowling Green)
Hughes, Harry E. (Bowling Green)
Hughes, H. Henry (Bowling Green)
Hughes, Rollie H. (Bowling Green)
Hull, Claud (Prairie Depot)
Hull, Weldon H. (Prairie Depot)
Hunter, William D. (Bowling Green)
Huss, Gordon V. (Luckey)
Husted, Clarence H. (Weston)
Husted, Lester Morison (Weston)
Husted, Roy Thomas (Weston)
Huston, Earl Levi (Bowling Green)
Huston, Glen (Haskins)
Hutton, Robert R., Jr. (Bradner)

I

Ilen, W.E. (Rossford)
Ireland, Albert (Bowling Green)
Ireland, Milton A. (Bowling Green)
Ireland, William (Bowling Green)
Isch, Arnold Fredrick (Walbridge)

J

Jacobs, Lawrence E (Maumee)
Jeffrey, James Jasper Garfield (Weston)
Jeffrey, Raymond Sherman (Dunbridge)
Jenkins, Harry E. (Pemberville)
Jewell, Ivan D. (Bowling Green)
Jimison, Floyd R. (North Baltimore)

Jimison, Perry Hiram (North Baltimore)
Johnson, Adam (Weston)
Johnson, Albert S. (Bowling Green)
Johnson, Clayton A. (Bowling Green)
Johnson, Howard C. (North Baltimore)
Johnson, Howard E. (Bowling Green)
Johnson, Hubert Ellis (Perrysburg)
Johnson, John G. (Pemberville)
Johnson, Otto H. (Portage)
Johnston, Earl Walter (Rudolph)
Johnston, Harold A. (Bowling Green)
Johnston, Henry P (North Baltimore)
Johnston, John W. (Prairie Depot)
Johnston, Wilson J. (Bowling Green)
Jones, Albert S. (Rudolph)
Jones, Allen H. (Rossford)
Jones, D.H. (Rossford)
Jones, Harold H. (Rudolph)
Jones, Hugh H. (Rossford)
Jones, Orton Hobart (Bowling Green)
Jones, Vern Leroy (Rossford)
Jones, Virgil M. (Portage)
Joseph, Chester (Bowling Green)
Jurgens, August Johann (Luckey)

K

Kapp, Joe G. (East Toledo)
Kapp, Ray F. (East Toledo)
Karns, Jay (Haskins)
Keller, Amos (Rudolph)
Keller, August "Gus" F. (Bowling Green)
Kelley, Clair Taylor (North Baltimore)
Kelley, Curtis E. (North Baltimore)
Kelly, John Edson (Bowling Green)
Kelsey, Wade Hampton (Weston)
Kerr, Emmett (Cygnet)
Ketzenbarger, Earl W. (Bowling Green)
Ketzenbarger, Emory Lee (Bowling Green)
Kidney, Ralph L. (Perrysburg)
Kieffer, D.T. (Milton Center)
Kieffer, Wilbur McKinley (Rudolph)
Killian, Calvin R. (Maumee)
Killian, Howard C. (Portage)

Killian, John L. (Bowling Green)
Kimmons, Fred (Bowling Green)
King, Alfred (Bellevue)
King, Bert W. (Perrysburg)
King, Dale M. (Haskins)
King, Frank E (Cygnet)
King, Walter Edward (Rossford)
Kinney, Quincy A. (Mermill)
Kinsey, Albert H. (Prairie Depot)
Kinsey, Harvey (Prairie Depot)
Kistler, Elmer G. (Perrysburg)
Kistner, Charles W. (Bowling Green)
Kitchen, Fred L. (Bowling Green)
Kline, Fay Hobson (Deshler)
Kline, Forrester Edward (Deshler)
Knaggs, George C. (Portage)
Knepley, Ernest O. (Bowling Green)
Knouss, George T. (Weston)
Knull, Harry M. (Bowling Green)
Kompe, Clair (Bowling Green)
Koons, Alva W. (Bowling Green)
Koons, Charles Alfred (Bairdstown)
Koons, Jay C. (Bowling Green)
Kramer, Jack W. (Bowling Green)
Krassow, Christopher Joseph (Portage)
Krauss (Knauss), Jay (Fremont)
Krontz, Delbert Charles (Rudolph)
Krontz, Virgil L. (Rudolph)
Krouse, Floyd J. (Prairie Depot)
Krouse, Harley L. (North Baltimore)
Krutsch, Bert (North Baltimore)

l

Ladd, George A. (Weston)
Ladell, Lloyd W. (Bowling Green)
Lahman, William Franklin (Bowling Green)
Lamb, G.W. (Rossford)
Lambright, Floyd J. (Bloomdale)
Lance, Abraham H. (Weston)
Lance, David (Milton Center)
Lance, James Frederick (Weston)
Landis, Clark A. (Bowling Green)
Lane, Joe (Bowling Green)
Laney, Jay W. (North Baltimore)

Laney, Thomas Corwin (North Baltimore)
Laremore, Lance E. (Bowling Green)
Laremore, J.H. (Bowling Green)
Lashway, Stanley E. (Bowling Green)
Lauker, R.B. (Grand Rapids)
Laurer, Frank (Rossford)
Lawrence, Dallas D. (Bowling Green)
Lawrence, Parley G. (Toledo)
Leathers, Ed (Perrysburg)
Leathers, Edward L. (Bowling Green)
Lee, Charles F. (Bowling Green)
Lee, Howard E. (Bowling Green)
Lee, Joseph "Jay" L. (Bowling Green)
Lee, Joseph Leroy (Bowling Green)
Lee, Thomas E. (Bowling Green)
Legalley, H. B. (Bowling Green)
Lehman, Charles R. (Custar)
Lein, Walter Leroy (Portage)
Leiter, Cyril Faun (Fawn) (Findlay)
Leiter, Earl R. (Bowling Green)
Leiter, Seneca S. (Bowling Green)
Leslie, Levi (Cygnet)
Levers, Daniel W. (Weston)
Leverton, Merle (Bowling Green)
Leydorf, Chistian C (Perrysburg)
Leydorf, William C. (Perrysburg)
Limestall, C.F. (Bowling Green)
Limmer, Albert John (Perrysburg)
Limmer, Arnold G. (Perrysburg)
Limmer, Edgar John (Haskins)
Lindquist, Guy (Hoytville)
Lingo, Harry Leroy (Milton Center)
Linkenstine, Harold E. (Bowling Green)
Locke, Norman W. (Bowling Green)
Lodge, Arthur Homes (Bowling Green)
Long, Harry A. (Bowling Green)
Long, Howard M. (Weston)
Long, Merle L. (Bowling Green)
Longacre, George Henry (Cygnet)
Longbrake, Walter A. (Milton Center)
Longwell, Addison B (Bowling Green)
Loomis, Clyde A. (Bowling Green)
Loomis, Roy E. (Bowling Green)
Loop, Clint Elmer (Walbridge)

Loop, Curtis Allen (Rossford)
Loop, Melvin G. (Walbridge)
Loose, Nathaniel E (Bowling Green)
Lowe, Bernard (Bowling Green)
Lowe, William A. (Bowling Green)
Luce, Elmer J. (Portage)
Ludwig, George Arthur Sr. (Rudolph)
Luebben, Fredrick William (Perrysburg)
Lusher, Raymond D. (Perrysburg)
Lytle, Joseph E. (Haskins)
Lytle, Ralph (Bowling Green)

M

Madden, Alanzo W. (Toledo)
Maddock, William (Rossford)
Mahler, Harley H. (Bowling Green)
Mallon, James (Perrysburg)
Mandell, Raymond A. (Perrysburg)
Mann, Nelson J. (Milton Center)
Mansfield, Ross G. (Rudolph)
Mansfield, William V. (Rudolph)
Mantel, Sherman Sylvester (Weston)
Marks, Ernest J. (Bowling Green)
Marriott, Elmer G. (Maumee)
Marsh, Lawton Wade (Bowling Green)
Martin, Charles "Charley" H. (Prairie
   Depot)
Martin, Charles E. (Prairie Depot)
Martin, George H. (Bowling Green)
Martin, Milo (Prairie Depot)
Martin, Nelson B. (Prairie Depot)
Mason, Lester E (Bowling Green)
Matheney, Charles Alexander
   (Walbridge)
Matheney, Wilfred T. (Walbridge)
Matheny, Jess Barrett (Rudolph)
Mathis, Little Fletcher (Bowling Green)
Maxwell, Edward (Bowling Green)
Maynard, William S. (Bowling Green)
Mays, Grant (North Baltimore)
McBride, Gerald D. (Maumee)
McCauley, Herbert A. (Bowling Green)
McClay, David W. (Bowling Green)
McClure, Frank W. (Mermill)

McCormick, George William (Prairie
   Depot)
McCoy, Cecil (Pemberville)
McCrary, C.C. (Toledo)
McCreary, Ray M. (Bowling Green)
McCrory, Charles A. (Bowling Green)
McCrory, Irvin (Bowling Green)
McCrory, Samuel L. (Weston)
McDonald, J.B. (Rudolph)
McElroy, Jesse (Jess) R. (Bowling Green)
McGuire, James J. (Rudolph)
McKenzie, Clyde W. (Bowling Green)
McLaughlin, James H. (North
   Baltimore)
McMahan, Charles Ober (Jerry City)
McMahon, D.D. (Cygnet)
McMan, William R. (Bowling Green)
McMann, Rolla D. (Bowling Green)
Mead, Arthur C (Bowling Green)
Means, James J., Jr. (Portage)
Meeker, Alton Chester (Bowling Green)
Mercer, Charles Tilton (North
   Baltimore)
Mercer, Frank B. (North Baltimore)
Mercer, Frank H. (Rudolph)
Mercer, Harry W. (Weston)
Mercer, Lorenzo D. (Bowling Green)
Mercer, Owen E. (Weston)
Mercer, Samuel A. (Weston)
Mericle, John H. (Perrysburg)
Mettler, Fred W. (Hoytville)
Meyer, Edwin C. (North Baltimore)
Meyer, J.E. (North Baltimore)
Michelsen, Christ Hans (Stony Ridge)
Miller, Anthony A. (North Baltimore)
Miller, Christie (Bowling Green)
Miller, C.L. (Luckey)
Miller, David L. (Bloomdale)
Miller, Dean (Bowling Green)
Miller, Grover C. (Bowling Green)
Miller, John Franklin (Bowling Green)
Miller, Paul (Weston)
Miller, Vernon "Vern" E. (Weston)
Miller, William R. (Grand Rapids)
Mills, Charles J. (Bowling Green)

Mills, Glee W. (Bowling Green)
Mills, Warren F. (Bowling Green)
Milnor, Harold T. (Bowling Green)
Milnor, William W. (Bowling Green)
Miner, Hugh (Tontogany)
Mintz, H. B. (Rossford)
Miser, Clarence W. (Grand Rapids)
Monasmith, Elias Hewitt (North Baltimore)
Montague, William O. (North Baltimore)
Moore, George S. (North Baltimore)
Moore, Joseph H. (Rudolph)
Moore, T.C. (Rudolph)
Morehead, J.D. (North Baltimore)
Morrison, Kelly Love (Perrysburg)
Morrison, William E. (Fostoria)
Mortimer, Martin Ellsworth (North Baltimore)
Moser, Ernest W. (Perrysburg)
Muir, DeFrehn T. (Perrysburg)
Mundwiler, Olen Harold (Hoytville)
Munn, Cloyse H. (Bowling Green)
Munsel, Morgan S. (Bowling Green)
Munson, Levi (Toledo)
Murdock, C.W. (Haskins)
Murdock, Earl (Bowling Green)
Murlin, Harry E. (Bowling Green)
Murphey, Samuel "Sam" Alan (Weston)
Musser, F. Vane (Pemberville)
Musser, H.L. (Genoa)
Musser, Ruben M. (Pemberville)
Mutchler, Elmer A. (Rossford)
Myers, A.F. (Bowling Green)
Myers, George L. (North Baltimore)
Myers, Leon Leonidis (Bowling Green)
Myers, Myron (Custar)
Myers, Orley W. (Bowling Green)
Myers, Rolley R. (Cygnet)

N

Nangle [Naugle], Charles H. (Bowling Green)
Neal, George S. (Cygnet)
Neff, Willis Forry (Risingsun)

Nelson, Oscar (Portage)
Newman, Cecil I. (Bowling Green)
Newton, James (Walbridge)
Ney, Edward Campbell (Weston)
Nichols, Frank C. (North Baltimore)
Nichols, James A. (North Baltimore)
Nichols, Ralph O. (North Baltimore)
Nietz, John Alfred (Perrysburg)
Nissen, Carl Martin (Lime City)
Nixon, Clarence Henry (Pemberville)
Nobles, Melvin (East Toledo)
Nolenberger, George H. (Perrysburg)
Norris, Charles E. (Bowling Green)
North, Francis I. (Haskins)
Noyes, Charles T. (Bowling Green)
Noyes, Claire M. (Bowling Green)

O

Oates, Wilbur S. (Rossford)
Oats, Ralph W. (Cygnet)
Older, Michael Boyer (Bowling Green)
Ollendorf, William (Bowling Green)
O'Neal, Charles Samuel (Weston)
O'Neal, Harry Sylvester (Weston)
O'Neal, John Edward (Weston)
O'Neal, William McKinley (Weston)
O'Neill, Russell (Portage)
Osborn, Clyde (Bowling Green)
Osborn, Harrison Peter (Bowling Green)
Osborn, J. Arthur (Bowling Green)
Osborn, Vincent B. (Weston)
Osborne, North G. (Bowling Green)
Osborne, William E. (Rudolph)
Otley, Benjamin M (Bowling Green)
Otley, Clifford (Bowling Green)
Overmyer, Nathaniel (Walbridge)

P

Packard, Lowell Delss (Milton Center)
Page, Charles Ebeneezer (Rossford)
Pair, Lester M. (Perrysburg)
Park, Lehr (Lerve) Ralph (Bowling Green)
Parsons, H.M. (Portage)

Parsons, Scott R. (Portage)
Patrick, Guy C. (Findlay)
Patterson, Edgar Earnest (Rudolph)
Patterson, Harry B. (Rudolph)
Patterson, Mellville Jacob (North Baltimore)
Payne, F.G. (Grand Rapids)
Peinert, Harold E. (Haskins)
Peinert, William F. (Weston)
Pennock, George Whipple (Weston)
Pennybacker, Perry L. (Bowling Green)
Peoples, Garver Allen (Portage)
Perkins, George Edward (Perrysburg)
Perrine, Lawrence V. (Bloomdale)
Perry, Glode, Jr. (Rudolph)
Perry, William Augustus (Cygnet)
Peterson, Arthur (Perrysburg)
Peterson, David "Pete" Peter (Bowling Green)
Peterson, John C. (Lime City)
Petty, Fred M. (Bowling Green)
Pfisterer, Conrad Martin (Toledo)
Phelps, Charles Edward (Weston)
Phelps, Charles Glenn (Weston)
Philbin, Phillip A. (Rossford)
Phillips, Arthur (Tontogany)
Phillips, Aldace John (Tontogany)
Phillips, Claud (North Baltimore)
Phillips, Jay (Tontogany)
Phillips, John D., Sr., Bowling Green)
Phillips, Joseph R (North Baltimore)
Phillips, Seth D. (Bowling Green)
Phillips, Thomas B. (Perrysburg)
Piddock, Floyd E. (Portage)
Pierce, E.H. (Bowling Green)
Pierce, D.A. (Radcliff)
Plotner, Paul (Bowling Green)
Plouck, Delmar Russell (Mermill)
Plouck, Harry (Mermill)
Plouck, Sherman R. (Mermill)
Poland, Donovan (Bowling Green)
Porter, Archer "Archie" Henry (Weston)
Potter, Ray V. (Weston)
Potterfield, Lee Shires (Rossford)
Powell, Rush Augustus (Bowling Green)

Powers, Jesse E. (Bowling Green)
Powers, William (Walbridge)
Prentice, Harry K. (Bowling Green)
Preston, Louis D. (Pemberville)
Priest, Norman Andrew (Custar)
Pringle, Jacob "Joe" (Perrysburg)
Pringle, Lano (Rossford)
Pringle, Sanford P. (Rossford)
Prowant, Clarence E. (Bowling Green)
Pruden, Charles Edgar (Haskins)
Pugh, Thomas J. (Weston)
Pugh, M.A. (Seneca Co.)
Pultz, David Newton (Rudolph)
Purvis, Norris (Perrysburg)

R

Rader, Edward H. (Cygnet)
Randall, Arthur K (Bowling Green)
Randall, Floyd (Mermill)
Raubenolt, Lloyd Lin (Weston)
Ray, George Emrick (Rudolph)
Ray, James H. (Rudolph)
Reed, Donald Boswell (Sugar Ridge)
Reed, Joseph Henry (Sugar Ridge)
Reed, Reuben Emanuel (Bowling Green)
Reeg, Cloyd M. (Toledo)
Reese, C.A. (Prairie Depot)
Reese, Clarence L. (Prairie Depot)
Remmel, John (Maumee)
Rhoades, Charles W. (Walbridge)
Rice, William H. (Tontogany)
Richard, Donald L. (Bowling Green)
Richard, Gerald F. (North Baltimore)
Richardson, Charles H. (Custar)
Richardson, Henry A. (Rudolph)
Rickard, C.H. (Bowling Green)
Rickett, Frank (Bowling Green)
Rickett, Ira L. (Bowling Green)
Ridgeway, Cordie Monroe (Bowling Green)
Riegle, John P. (Bowling Green)
Riegle, Theodore F. (Bowling Green)
Riess, Lynn Chester (Bowling Green)
Riggle, Chalmer B. (Perrysburg)

Rinker, George C. (Perrysburg)
Roach, Clark J. (Waterville)
Roach, Isaac B. (Bowling Green)
Robertson, Charles W. (Perrysburg)
Robertson, Ranald (Ronald) Lelia
(Haskins)
Robinson, Bruce E. (Rudolph)
Robinson, Henry "Hank" Clifford
(Haskins)
Robinson, Lee (Walbridge)
Robinson, Ross R. (Tontogany)
Robinson, William D. (Rudolph)
Robrahn, Walter (Walbridge)
Roe, B.D. (Weston)
Roe, R.B. (Bowling Green)
Roebke, William R. (Bowling Green)
Roether, Herbert Ewing (Perrysburg)
Roger, Lawrence J. (Weston)
Rogers, Frank W. (Bowling Green)
Rood, Alfred A. (Bowling Green)
Rood, Harold (Bowling Green)
Rood, Lewis Leroy (Bowling Green)
Rood, John H. (Bowling Green)
Rood, Joseph M., Sr. (Bowling Green)
Rosendale, Ben H. (North Baltimore)
Ross, Elmer E. (Rudolph)
Ross, Floyd O. (Rudolph)
Ross, Reynolds D. (Rudolph)
Rouse, F. Lee (Bowling Green)
Routson, Elmer E. (Bowling Green)
Rubley, William P. (Perrysburg)
Rugh, Elmer C. (Bowling Green)
Rundlett, Warren M. (Mermill)
Runyon, Earl Cleo (Stony Ridge)
Russell, Edward F. (Bowling Green)
Rutledge, Calvin C. (Bowling Green)

S

Sanderson, Ernest Edwin (Prairie
Depot)
Sanford, Edward M. (Rudolph)
Sangston, William W. (Bowling Green)
Santmire, Merle Watson (Bairdstown)
Sarver, Forest E. (Rossford)
Sasse, Fred W. (Perrysburg)

Sawyer, Clarence N. (Rossford)
Sawyer, Herbert (Rossford)
Schaller, Andrew (Perrysburg)
Schaller, Elmer R. (Perrysburg)
Schaller, Ernest (Perrysburg)
Schauwaker, Howard A. (Bowling
Green)
Schauweker, Wilber Wayne (Portage)
Scheider, Elmer George (Perrysburg)
Scheider, Fred John (Perrysburg)
Schlicher, Burton Jacob (Bowling
Green)
Schlyer, Christopher H. (Milton Center)
Schroyer, F.L. (Prairie Depot)
Schuler, Reuben C. (Bowling Green)
Schumacher, Fred W. (Dunbridge)
Schumaker, Carl W. (Dowling)
Schumaker, Loyd (Bowling Green)
Schwab, Alex Andrew (North
Baltimore)
Schwab, Charles E. (Bowling Green)
Schwartz, Earnest (Rossford)
Scott, George Franklin (North
Baltimore)
Seibert, C.B. (Weston)
Seibert, Charles (North Baltimore)
Seiple, Frank J. (Bowling Green)
Seiple, Milton L. (Bowling Green)
Sewell, Herbert Clarence (North
Baltimore)
Shade, Monroe F. (Lime City)
Shane, George W. (Cygnet)
Shanower, Otis Carl (Bowling Green)
Sharp, Lewis R. (Bowling Green)
Shedenhelm, Ulysses E. (Prairie Depot)
Sheets, Arnold Jackson (Pemberville)
Sheldrick, Harry J. (Lime City)
Sheline, Elza Ray (Bowling Green)
Sheline, Isaac (Portage)
Sheperd, Norman W. (Tontogany)
Shepperd, Stephen L. (Perrysburg)
Sherer, Glen E. (Bowling Green)
Sherer, Harvey Hanford (Bowling
Green)
Sherer, Marshall Ney (Bowling Green)

Appendix I

Sherman, Carl I. (Portage)
Sherman, Charles L. (Portage)
Sherman, Lester Ernest (Portage)
Sherward, Eugene W. (Pemberville)
Shetzer, Floyd (Portage)
Shinew, James Wilson (Rudolph)
Shipman, Charles L. (Weston)
Shipman, Harry R. (Toledo)
Shirey, John A. (Rudolph)
Shirley, Oliver H (Rossford)
Shockey, Ray B. (Rudolph)
Shockey, Tracy L. (Rudolph)
Shoe, William Dale (Perrysburg)
Shoe, William W. (Perrysburg)
Shoup, Charles J. (Rudolph)
Shoup, Matt E. (Rudolph)
Shrier, John A. (Perrysburg)
Shrier, Melvin H. (Perrysburg)
Shroyer, Arthur G. (Portage)
Shroyer, Olen J. (Weston)
Shroyer, Oliver G. (Weston)
Shuman, Frederick (Bowling Green)
Sibler, T.W. (Bowling Green)
Siegling, Edmond M. (Bowling Green)
Sigler, Ray (Walbridge)
Simmons, Dale (Bowling Green)
Simmons, John A. (Dowling)
Simon, Floyd (North Baltimore)
Simon, Guy (North Baltimore)
Simon, Herman (Bloomdale)
Sims, Frank (Bowling Green)
Singleton, Grover S. (Cygnet)
Sites, Omar Dale (North Baltimore)
Sizemore, Robert (Rossford)
Slane, Venton [Vinton] G. (Rudolph)
Slane, Warren E. (Rudolph)
Slaughterbeck, Charles Ancil (North
    Baltimore)
Slaughterbeck, Floyd Leroy (North
    Baltimore)
Slaughterback, G.D. (Bowling Green)
Slaughterbeck, R.H. (Bloomdale)
Slawson, Fred C. (Bowling Green)
Slike, Leroy Vernon (Cygnet)
Sloane, Vernon E. (Perrysburg)

Sly, Sanford Lloyd (Rudolph)
Small, Leslie M. (Rossford)
Smelser, Jesse D. (Bowling Green)
Smith, Asa (North Baltimore)
Smith, Bennett G. (Luckey)
Smith, Claude A. (Bowling Green)
Smith, Claude B. (Bowling Green)
Smith, Earl D. (Bowling Green)
Smith, Earl "Pete" Dewey (Rudolph)
Smith, Emmanuel A. (Bowling Green)
Smith, Frank E. (Bowling Green)
Smith, Fred G. (North Baltimore)
Smith, Isaac Dallas (North Baltimore)
Smith, James G. (Bowling Green)
Smith, James R., Jr. (Rudolph)
Smith, John E. (Rudolph)
Smith, John W. (Bowling Green)
Smith, Lee A. (Pemberville)
Smith, Roy H. (North Baltimore)
Snow, Charles P. (Portage)
Snow, William Henry (Portage)
Snyder, Allen C. (Rossford)
Snyder, Amos B. (Walbridge)
Snyder, Charles Ernest (North
    Baltimore)
Snyder, Christian W. (Dunbridge)
Snyder, Eugene F. (Perrysburg)
Snyder, F.M. (Bradner)
Snyder, Fredrick Austin (Tontogany)
Snyder, G.G. (Prairie Depot)
Snyder, Henry L. (Findlay)
Snyder, Russell R. (Perrysburg)
Snyder, Wilson L. (Rudolph)
Sommer, Sylverius G. (Bowling Green)
Sommers, Jacob John (North Baltimore)
Spathelf, Owen W. (Tontogany)
Speaker, Harley J. (Rudolph)
Spencer, Raymond J. (Bowling Green)
Spilker, Benjamin F. (Perrysburg)
Spilker, Carl Emerson (Perrysburg)
Spilker, Edward J. (Perrysburg)
Spitler, Dan B. (Hoytville)
Spreng, Harry Hartzler (Perrysburg)
Springer, Philip (Rossford)
Stackhouse, William (Rossford)

Stage, Leo Denzle (Weston)
Stahl, P.J. (Prairie Depot)
Stahl, Roy (Risingsun)
Stammel, W.E. (Hoytville)
Staver, Harold B. (North Baltimore)
Stein, Andrew V. (Walbridge)
Stein, Wint M. (Walbridge)
Sterling, Herbert C. (Grand Rapids)
Sterling, James H. (North Baltimore)
Sterling, Joe Elmer (North Baltimore)
Sterling, Paul W. (North Baltimore)
Sterling, Thomas S. (Grand Rapids)
Sterns, W.E. (Weston)
Stetzer, Franz Martin (North Baltimore)
Stevenson, William F. (Weston)
Steward, Homer (Rossford)
Steward, M. (Rossford)
Stewart, L.V. (Bowling Green)
Stickler, Richard (Perrysburg)
Stimmel, Herbert C. (Bowling Green)
Stitt, James M. (Bowling Green)
Stitt, John J. (Risingsun)
Stockwell, Albert Erwin (Rudolph)
Stockwell, Amandus Frederic (Rudolph)
Stockwell, George Edwin (Portage)
Stockwell, Ross B. (Rudolph)
Stockwell, Roy E. (Rudolph)
Stoddard, Ernest A. (Tontogany)
Stoddard, Donald D. (Weston)
Stoddard, Lee A. (Bowling Green)
Stoots, Floyd Cleo (Bowling Green)
Stout, Harry O. (Bowling Green)
Stovath, Ray (Weston)
Strouser, L.W. (Bowling Green)
Stuller, B.F. (Bowling Green)
Stuller, Leroy (Bowling Green)
Stuller, Lloyd (Bowling Green)
Stump, Walter Herbert (Grand Rapids)
Sullivan, George I. (Dowling)
Sutton, Royce A. (Bowling Green)
Swan, Eugene B (Bowling Green)
Swartz, Charles A. (North Baltimore)
Swartz, Sam (Perrysburg)
Swartz, Wilbur (Bowling Green)
Sweet, Clarence A. (North Baltimore)

Swindler, James "Les" Lester (Bowling Green)
Swindler, Merlen Ray (Bowling Green)
Swope, Emmett L. (North Baltimore)
Swope, Lavird S. (North Baltimore)
Swope, Ronald H. (North Baltimore)
Symonds, Carl E (Rudolph)
Symonds, Roy E. (North Baltimore)

T

Taylor, Gladwin (North Baltimore)
Thompson, Hobart E. (Rudolph)
Thompson, James L. (Rudolph)
Thornton, John H. (Perrysburg)
Thornton, Ora W. (Walbridge)
Thorton, Claude (Rossford)
Thurman, Leland Burton (Weston)
Thurman, Roscoe James (Rudolph)
Thurston, Stanley M. (Bowling Green)
Tolles, Earl F. (Weston)
Tolles, Fred C. (Weston)
Towers, Harry (Bowling Green)
Trautman, George W. (North Baltimore)
Treece, Orin Clive (Perrysburg)
Triggs, William C. (Weston)
Troutner, Arthur Burton (Bowling Green)
Trumbull, Claud Emmett (Milton Center)
Turner, Sidney J. (Bowling Green)
Tyson, Charles D. (Prairie Depot)
Tyson, Sylvanus E. (Bowling Green)

U

Uhrig, Robert Eugene (Bowling Green)
Underdown, William John Ephraim (Mermill)
Underwood, Earl Lesley (Weston)
Underwood, Samuel Wright (Custar)
Urschell, Harold C. (Bowling Green)
Uthoff, Elmo R. (Perrysburg)

V

Valentine, Sam (Bowling Green)
Van Eman, John L. (Bloomdale)
Van Norman, Harrison "Harry" Edwin (Weston)
Van Voorhis, Hiram N. (Bowling Green)
Van Vorce, Carl Benton (North Baltimore)
Vanaman, Charles Robert (North Baltimore)
Vaughn, Paul W. (North Baltimore)
Vogelsong, H. (Prairie Depot)
Vollmar, Ephraim (Tontogany)
Vollmar, E. Roy (Haskins)
Vollmar, Frank (Tontogany)
Vollmar, John (Tontogany)
Volmer, Ray A. (Haskins)

W

Wade, Frank J. (Weston)
Wade, Joseph W. (Grand Rapids)
Wagner, Dewey E. (North Baltimore)
Wagner, Foster Charles (Bowling Green)
Wagner, G.C. (Bowling Green)
Wagner, Hamby (Hoytville)
Wagner, Noah (Hoytville)
Wagoner, O.J. (Bowling Green)
Walden, Alfred E. (Portage)
Walgamuth, Albert (Cygnet)
Walker, Ariel H. (Bowling Green)
Walker, Deloy F. (Bowling Green)
Walker, John B. (Perrysburg)
Walker, Ralph J. (Weston)
Wallace, Robert "Lew" Lewis (Sugar Ridge)
Wambold, Edward O. (Toledo)
Warfel, Herbert E. (Bowling Green)
Warren, William G. (Bowling Green)
Waters, Romer R. (Perrysburg)
Watkins, John F. (Toledo)
Waugh, Harold W. (Portage)
Waugh, Herbert Herman (Grand Rapids)
Waugh, Walter D. (Bowling Green)
Waugh, William W. (Bowling Green)
Weaver, Earl W. (Perrysburg)
Webster, Bratche Agee (Perrysburg)
Weirough, George (North Baltimore)
Welch, Harry E. (Bowling Green)
Weller, Norman Ross (Bloomdale)
Wells, Harley M. (Perrysburg)
Wellstead, Carl F. (Perrysburg)
Weng, Emery E. (Haskins)
Wenig, Gordon J. (Haskins)
Wenkel, L.W. (Rossford)
Wescott, William Noble (Perrysburg)
West, Clinton (Bowling Green)
Westcott, F (Perrysburg)
Whitacre, Carl E. (Cygnet)
Whitacre, Herman W. (Cygnet)
Whitacre, Reason Hayes (Rudolph)
White, William H. (Bowling Green)
Whitehead, E.H. (Bowling Green)
Whitehead, Walter J. (Milton Center)
Whitker, Royce Albert (Bowling Green)
Whitman, Charles F. (Custar)
Whitman, Laurel E. (Maumee)
Whitmer, Fred (Bowling Green)
Whitmill, Earl D. (Bowling Green)
Whitney, Walter Jay (Weston)
Whittmer, Robert Ray (Bowling Green)
Wichner, Frederick William (North Baltimore)
Wickham, Earl William (Bowling Green)
Wierick, Otis E. (Bloomdale)
Wight, Leonard Evan (Pemberville)
Wilch, John W. (Bloomdale)
Wilcox, J.B. (Bowling Green)
Wildman, Thomas W. (Bairdstown)
Wilkinson, Marcus Alva (North Baltimore)
Williams, Charles W. (Bowling Green)
Williams, Edward A. (Tontogany)
Williams, J.A. (Rudolph)
Williams, James M. (Rossford)
Williams, R.S. (Grand Rapids)
Wilson, Harold S. (Bowling Green)

Appendix I

Wilson, Hugh D. (Custar)
Wilson, M.A. (Bowling Green)
Wilson, Raleigh A. (North Baltimore)
Winbigler, William Wilson (North Baltimore)
Winters, Charles M. (Custar)
Winters, James R. (Custar)
Wintersteen, Ernest L. (Toledo)
Wires, Fred H. (Tontogany)
Wires, John W. (Tontogany)
Wirt, Wilber Lewis (North Baltimore)
Wisely, Marion S. (Bowling Green)
Witherald, G.A. (Toledo)
Withrow, Forest Everett (Weston)
Withrow, Ottis D. (North Baltimore)
Witte, Raymond F. (Rossford)
Witzler, Charles Mann (Perrysburg)
Woessner, John H. (Perrysburg)
Wolf, Charles E. (Prairie Depot)
Wolf, Oscar (Pemberville)
Wolfe, Charles E. (Rudolph)
Wood, Arnold (Bowling Green)
Wood, Arthur, Sr. (Bowling Green)
Wood, C.A. (Maumee)
Wood, Loren L. (Bowling Green)
Wood, William H. (Bowling Green)
Woodruff, Enoc, W., Jr. (Prairie Depot)
Wright, Bland O. (Bowling Green)
Wright, Ira Everett (Cygnet)
Wyer, Rufus M. (Prairie Depot)
Wymer, John E. (North Baltimore)

Y

Yates, J.C. (Bloomdale)
Yeager, John Oran (Perrysburg)
Yoder, Richard R. (Pemberville)
Yoder, Zachary (Zachariah) H. (Prairie Depot)
Young, A.C. (Bowling Green)
Young, A.E. (Prairie Depot)
Young, Albert R. (Bowling Green)
Young, Clark M. (Bowling Green)
Young, H.M. (Prairie Depot)
Young, Jacob W. (Portage)

Young, Martin Earl (Bowling Green)
Younkin, Russell M. (Bowling Green)

Z

Zimmerman, John (Bowling Green)
Zink, Delphan G. (North Baltimore)
Zink, Orlo James (Cygnet)
Zissler, Clarence E. (Tontogany)

WOOD COUNTY KLAN NEW INITIATE OATH CEREMONY

GOD GIVE US MEN

God Give Us Men! The Invisible Empire demands
Strong minds, great hearts, true faith and ready hands.
Men whom the lust for office does not kill;
Men whom the spoils of office cannot buy;
Men who possess opinions and a will;
Men who have honor; men who will not lie;
Men who can stand before a demagogue and damn his treacherous flattering
without winking!
Tall men, sun crowned, who live above the fog
In public duty and private thinking;
For while the rabble, with their thumb-worn creeds,
Their large professions and little deeds,
Mingle in selfish strife, Lo freedom weeps,
Wrong rules the land, and waiting justice sleeps,
God give us men!
Men who serve not for selfish booty,
But real men, courageous, who flinch not at duty;
Men of dependable character; men of sterling worth;
Then wrongs will be redressed, and right will rule the earth.
God Give Us Men!

QUALIFYING INTERROGATORIES

Sirs, the Knights of the Ku Klux Klan, as a great and essetially [*sic*] a patriotic, fraternal, and benevolent order, does not discriminate against a man on account of his religious or political creed when [the] same does not conflict with or antagonize the sacred rights and privileges guaranteed by our civil government and christian [*sic*] ideals and institutions.

Therefore to avoid any misunderstanding and as evidnece [*sic*] that we do not seek to impose unjustly the requirements of this order upon anyone who can not [*sic*], on account of his political or religious scruples, voluntarily meet our requirements or not, we require as an absolute necessity on the part of each of you an affirmative answer to each of the following questions:

Is the motive prompting your ambition to be a Klansman serious and unselfish?

Are you a white, Gentile, American Citizen?

Are you absolutely opposed to and free from any allegiance od [*sic*] any nature to any cause, Government, people, sect or ruler that is foreign to the United States of America?

Do you believe in the tenets of the christian [*sic*] religion?

Do you esteem the United States of America and it's [*sic*] institutions above any other government, civil, political, or ecclesiastical, in the whole world?

Will you without reservation take the solemn oath to defend, preserve, and enforce same?

Do you believe in Klanishness [*sic*] and will you faithfully practice same towards Klansmen?

Do you believe in and will you faithfully strive for the eternal maintenance of white supremacy?

Will you faithfully obey our constitution and laws and conform willingly to all our usages, requirements, and regulations?

Can you always be depended on?

SECTION 1

You will place your left hand over your heart and raise your right hand to heaven.

You will say "I"—pronounce your name in full—and repeat after me—in the presence of God and Man—most solemnly pledge, promise and swear—unconditionally—that I will faithfully obey—the constitution and laws—and will willingly conform to—all regulations, useges [*sic*], and requirements—of the [Klan] which do now exist—or which may be hereafter enacted—and will render at all times—loyal respect and stedfast [*sic*] support—to the Imperial authority of same—and will heartily heed—all official mandates—decrees—edicts—rulings and instructions—of the I*W* [Imperial Wizard?] thereof.—I will yield prompt responce [*sic*]—to all summondses [*sic*]—I having knowledge of same—Providence alone preventing.

SECTION 2

I most solemnly swear—that I will forever—Keep sacredly secret—the signes [*sic*] words and grips—and any and all other—matters and kneowledge [*sic*] of the [Klan]—regarding which—a most rigid secrecy—must be maintained. Which may at any time—be communicated to me—and will never divulge same—nor even cause same to be divulged—toany [*sic*] person in the whole world—unless I know positively—that such person is a member of this order—in good and regular standing—and not even then—unless it be—for the best interest of the order.

I most sacredly vow—and most positively swear—that I never yield to bribe— flattery—threats—passion—punishment—persecution—nor any other eicene [*sic*] whatsoever—coming from or offered by—any person or persons—male or female—for thepurpose [*sic*] of—obtaining from me—a secret or secret information—of the [Klan]—I will die rather than divulge the same—so help me God—Amen.

You will lower your hands.

REAL FRATERNITY

Real Fraternity, by shamefull [*sic*] neglect, has been starved until so weak her voice is lost in the Courts of her own castle and she passes unnoticrd [*sic*] by her sworn subjects as she moves along the crowded streets and thru [*sic*] the din of the market places. Man's valuation of man is by the standard of wealth and not worth; selfishness is the festive queen among human kind and multitudes forget honor, justice, love, God and every religious conviction to do homage to her; and yet with the cruel heart of Jezebel, she slaughters the souls of thousands of her devoties [*sic*] daily.

The unsatisfied thirst for gain is dethroning reason and judgment in the citadel of the human soul and men madden thereby, for get [*sic*] their patriotic, domestic and social obligations and duties, and fiendishly fight for a place in the favor of [a] goddess of glittering gold; they starve their own souls and make sport of spiritual developments.

You will place your left hane [*sic*] over your heart and raise your right hand to heaven. You will say "I"—pronounce your name in full—and repeat after me—"Before God—and in the presence of—these mysterious Klansmen—on my sacred honor—do most solemnly and sincerely—pledge, promise and swear—that I will diligently guard—and faithfully foster—every interest of the [Klan] and will maintain it's [*sic*] social cast and dignity.

I swear that I will never recommend—and person for membership in this order— whose mind is unsound—whose reputation I know to be bad—whose character is doubtful—orwhose [*sic*] loyalty to our country—is an [*sic*] any way questionable."

SECTION 3

I swear that I will pay promptly—all just and legal demands—made upon me to defray the expenses—ofmy [*sic*] Klan and this order—when same are due or alled [*sic*] for.

I awear [*sic*] that I will protect the property—of the [Klan] —of any nature whatsoever—and if any should be intrusted [*sic*] to my keeping—I will properly keep—or rightfully use [the] same—and will freely and promptly surrender same—onoffical [*sic*] demand—orif [*sic*] ever I am banished from or volentarily [*sic*] discontinue—my mambership [*sic*] in this order.

I swear that I will most determinedly—maintain peace and harmony—in all the deliberations—of the gatherings or assemblies—of the [Klan]—or of any subordinate jurisdiction—or Klan thereof.

I swear I will most strenuously—discourage selfishness—and selfish political ambition—on the part of myself or any Klansman.

I swear that I will never allow—personal friendship—blood or family relationship—nor personal—political—or professional prejudice—malice—nor ill will—to influence me in casting my vote—for the election or rejection—of an applicant—for mambership [*sic*] in this order—God Being MY Helper.—Amen.

You will drop your hands.

CONGRATULATIONS

Sirs: We congratulate you on your manley [*sic*] decision to forsake the world of selfishness and fraternal alienation and emigrate [*sic*] to the delectable bonds of the

Invisable [*sic*] Enormous and become loyal citizens of the same. The prime purpose of this great order is the develop character, practice Klanishness [*sic*], to protect the home and the chastity of women-hood [*sic*], and to exeplify [*sic*] a pure patriotism towards our great country.

You as citizens of the Invisible Empire must be actively patriotic toward our country and constantly klanish [*sic*] toward Klansmen socially, physically normally and vocationally.

Will you assume this obligation of citizenship?

Sirs: if you have any doubts as to your ability to qualify, either in body of character as citizens of the Invisible Empire, you now have an opportunity to retire from this place with thw [*sic*] good will of the Klan to attend you; for I warn you now, if you falter or fail at this time or in the future as a Klansman, in Klonklave or in life, you will be banished from citizenship in the Invisible Empire without fear or favor.

This is a serious undertaking; we are not here to make sport of you nor indulge in the silly frivolity of circus clowns. Be you well assured that "He that putteth his hand to the plow and looketh back; is not fit for the kingdom of heaven" or worthy of the high honor of citizenship in the Invisable [*sic*] Empire, or the fervent fellowship of Klansmen. Don't deceive yourselves; you can not [*sic*] deceive us and we will not be mocked.

Do you wish to retire?

You will place your left hand over your heart and raise your right hand to heaven.

You will say "I"—pronounce your name in full—and repeat after me—that I will never slander—defraud—deceive—or in any manner wrong—the [Klan] —a Klansman—nor a Klansman's family—nor will I suffer the same to be done—if I can prevent it.

I swear that I will be faithful—in defending and protecting—the home— reputation—and physical and business interest—of a Klansman's family.

I swear that I will at all times—without hesitating—go to the assistance or rescue—of a Klansman in any way—at his call I will answer. I will be truly Klanish [*sic*] toward Klansmen in all things honorable.

I swear that I will never allow—any animosity—friction—nor ill will—to arise and remain—between myself and a Klansman—but will be constant in my efforts—to promote real Klanishness [*sic*]—among the members of this order.

I most solemnly promise and swear—that I will always—at all times and all places—help, aid and assist—the duly constituted officers of the law—in the proper performance of their legal duties.

I will keep secure to myself—a secret of a Klansman—when [the] same is committed to me—in the sacred bond of Klansmanship—The crime of violating this solemn oath—treason against the United States of America—rape—and malicious murder—alone excepted.

I most solemnly assert and affirm—that to the Government of the United States of America—and any state thereof—of which I may become a resident—I sacredly awear [*sic*]—an unqualifiedly allegiance—above any other and every kind of Government—in the whole world—I here and now pledge my life—my property—my vote and my sacred honor—to uphold it's [*sic*] flag—it's [*sic*] constitution and constitutional laws—and will protect—defend enforce same unto death.

I swear that I will most zealously—and valiantly—shield and preserve—by any and all—justifiable means and methods—the sacred constitutional rights—and privileges of free public schools—free speech—free press—seperation [*sic*] of church and state—liberty—white supremacy—just laws—and the pursuit of happiness—against any encroachment—of any nature—by any person or persons—political party or parties—religious sect or people—native, naturalized, or foreign—of any race—collor [*sic*]—creed—liniage [*sic*] of tongue whatever.

All to which I have sworn by this oath—I will seal with my blood—be thou my witness—Almighty God.—Amen.

You will drop your hands.

End of obligation.

NOTES

INTRODUCTION

1. *Wood County Republican*, "Klan Visit U.B. Church," February 14, 1923.
2. Ibid.

CHAPTER 1

3. *Perrysburg Journal*, "Teacher Held on Serious Charge," March 30, 1922.
4. *Wood County Republican*, "Mob Violence Attempted on Otto P. Tracy," May 13, 1922.
5. Ohio Department of Agriculture, Office of Farmland Preservation, *2012 Annual Report*, 13.
6. USDA National Agricultural Statistics Service, *2012 Ohio County Estimates*.
7. Ibid., *Wood County Profile*.
8. *Farm Journal*, 3.
9. Wood County Commissioners, "Guide to Wood County Government," 2.
10. *Black and Gold*, 8.
11. Bowling Green State University, "Enrollment History."
12. U.S. Census Bureau, *Wood County, Ohio*.
13. *Farm Journal*, 3.
14. *North Baltimore Times*, "Rossford: Small Town of Yesterday, Big City of Tomorrow—Prediction," March 21, 1924.
15. Ohio Federation of Churches, *Ohio Rural Church Survey*.
16. Ibid.
17. Warren, "Agricultural Depression," 200.
18. *Wood County Republican*, "What Farmers Need Costs More in 1924," September 25, 1924.

19. *Perrysburg Journal*, "Farmers Show Increasing Interest in State and National Affairs," January 15, 1920.

CHAPTER 2

20. *Daily Sentinel-Tribune*, "Ku Klux Klan Drew a Mammoth Crowd," October 5, 1923.
21. Ibid.
22. Some historians divide the third phase of the Klan into three smaller segments: a civil rights–era Klan from 1945 to 1970, the David Duke era from 1975 to 1985 and the millennial (or "Internet") Klan of the mid-1990s into the twenty-first century.
23. Lester, *Ku Klux Klan*, 60.
24. Dinnerstein, *Leo Frank Case*, 3–4.
25. Jackson, *Ku Klux Klan*, 10; Alexander, "Kleagles and Cash," 352.
26. Chalmers, *Hooded Americanism*, 175.
27. Lay, *Hooded Knights*, 4.
28. Ku Klux Klan, Inc., *America for Americans*, Atlanta, GA: 1922, 7.
29. *Wood County Republican*, "The Dangers of Illiteracy," September 11, 1924.
30. *New York Times*, "Ohio Governor Vetoes Bible Bill," May 1, 1925.
31. *Wood County Republican*, "Crime Cost Heavy in America," August 28, 1924.
32. Ku Klux Klan, Inc., *Should the Holy Bible Be Hidden*.
33. *Wood County Republican*, "Reasons Why Bible Reading Should be Practiced in the Public School," September 18, 1924.
34. *Wood County Republican*, "Huge Patriotic Meeting," July 26, 1923.

CHAPTER 3

35. *Perrysburg Journal*, January 8, 1920.
36. Ibid.
37. Ibid.
38. Ibid.
39. Ibid., January 15, 1920
40. Ibid.
41. Ibid.
42. Ibid., January 22, 1920.
43. Ibid.
44. Ibid.
45. Ibid.
46. Ibid.
47. Ibid., September 16, 1920.
48. *North Baltimore Times*, "Elks Minstrel Shows," March 30, 1923.
49. Ibid.
50. *Prairie Depot Observer*, "Darktown Strutters Ball," October 24, 1924.
51. *Bloomdale Derrick*, "Hoopla," November 21, 1924.

52. *Perrysburg Journal*, November 11, 1920.
53. *North Baltimore Times*, "Why He Wouldn't Come Up," February 2, 1923.
54. Ibid., "Return to Savage Habits," October 12, 1923.
55. *Wood County Democrat*, "Parker Found Guilty," February 16, 1923.
56. *Perrysburg Journal*, "State of the Negro," February 16, 1922.
57. Ibid.
58. *Wood County Democrat*, "Will Be Sent on His Way," January 5, 1923.
59. *Daily Sentinel-Tribune*, "Negro Arrested," August 2, 1923.
60. Ibid., "Big Rossford Fire," July 18, 1923.
61. Cincinnati Board of Education, Board Minutes, 514.
62. *Wood County Republican*, "Foreign Influence Threatens," September 18, 1924.
63. *Perrysburg Journal*, November 11, 1920.
64. Ibid., November 8, 1920.
65. Ibid.
66. *North Baltimore Times*, "Another Restricted Idea," September 21, 1923.
67. *Perrysburg Journal*, June 30, 1921.
68. Ibid.
69. Ibid., August 11, 1921.
70. *Wood County Republican*, "Deport the Bad Foreigner," July 12, 1923.
71. Ibid., "Rossford Ransacked for Illicit Booze," March 16, 1922.
72. *North Baltimore Times*, "Anarchists in Toledo," October 5, 1923.
73. *Wood County Republican*, "Crime Cost Heavy in America," August 28, 1924.
74. U.S. census 1920, Toledo, Ohio Ward 6, District 0076, sheet 5A.
75. *Wood County Republican*, "Rossford Raided Again," July 12, 1923.
76. *Daily Sentinel-Tribune*, "Chinese Grabbed at Rossford on Liquor Charge," July 10, 1923.
77. Ibid.
78. *North Baltimore Times*, "Good Business," November 23, 1923.
79. Ibid., "Probably a Klansman," November 16, 1923.
80. *Church of Rome in American Politics*, 3.
81. Ibid., 5.
82. Ibid., 39.
83. Ibid.
84. *Wood County Republican*, "The Relation of the Protestant Church to Citizenship," May 18, 1924.

CHAPTER 4

85. Ibid., "Charity Suffereth Long and is Kind," February 19, 1924.
86. Ibid.
87. Ibid.
88. Ibid.
89. Embrey Bernard Howson, *The Ku Klux Klan in Ohio After World War I*, 32.
90. *Cleveland Plain Dealer*, September 30, 1921.
91. *Columbus Dispatch*, August 30, 1925.

92. Records of Ohio Knights of the Ku Klux Klan, dues/membership record book, Center for Archival Collections, MS 731, box 1.

93. *Wood County Republican*, "Fiery Cross Is Burned by Klan," March 15, 1923.

94. Ibid., "Klan Doings in Wood County," August 14, 1923.

95. Annie E. Casey Foundation, *Changing Child Population*, 4.

96. McVeigh, "Structural Incentives," 1,471.

97. Horowitz, "Ku Klux Klan in LaGrande, Oregon," 195.

98. *Wood County Democrat*, "Klan Meetings," August 22, 1924.

99. *Daily Sentinel-Tribune*, "Ku Klux Klan Drew a Mammoth Crowd," October 5, 1923.

100. *Wood County Republican*, "Public Lecture at North Baltimore," June 5, 1924.

101. *Prairie Depot Observer*, "100 Percent American: Excellent Address Given by Rev. Wilch Monday Night," July 13, 1923.

102. "Kreed of the Women of the Ku Klux Klan," Center for Archival Collections, MS 731, box 2.

103. *Wood County Republican*, "Wood County Klan Soon to Charter," September 11, 1924.

104. *North Baltimore Times*, "Women's Klan," September 21, 1923.

105. *Wood County Republican*, "Klan Ladies Give Supper," March 6, 1924.

106. Ibid., "Lady Kluxers Made Donation," April 3, 1924.

107. Ibid., "Wood County Klonklave," October 30, 1924.

108. *North Baltimore Times*, "Klan Might Be Used Here," February 29, 1924.

CHAPTER 5

109. *Daily Sentinel-Tribune*, "That Explosion," August 15, 1923.

110. *New York Times*, "Klan Candidates Swept Ohio Cities," November 8, 1923.

111. Ibid.

112. *Akron Beacon Journal*, November 7, 1923.

113. *New York Times*, "Klan Candidates Swept Ohio Cities," November 8, 1923.

114. Ibid.

115. *Wood County Republican*, "To Close Business Places," July 5, 1923.

116. Ibid., "County G.O.P. Organizes," August 26, 1926.

117. *Black and Gold*, 58.

118. *Oracle*, 7.

119. *Bowling Green City Directory*, 237.

120. *Black and Gold*, 58.

121. "Teacher Training in the Secondary Schools," *Bowling Green Key*, 1934, 28.

122. "Faculty," *Hi-Echo*, 1923, 8.

123. *Literary Digest*, "For and Against the Ku Klux Klan," September 24, 1921.

124. Kevin F. Kern and Gregory S. Wilson, *Ohio: A History of the Buckeye State*, 367.

125. *Wood County Republican*, "Rossford Ransacked for Illicit Booze," March 16, 1923.

126. *Prairie Depot Observer*, "Disgrace to a Civilized Community," March 30, 1923.

127. *Wood County Republican*, "Klan Doings in Wood County," August 14, 1924.

128. Ibid., "Dry Federation Met," July 2, 1925.

129. Ibid.

130. Ibid., "Reverend R.A. Powell Senate Candidate," July 31, 1924.
131. *Wood County Democrat*, "The Sentinel Wrong Again," August 15, 1924.
132. Ibid.
133. Ibid., "Powell-Urschel" and "Klan Gathering," July 11, 1924.
134. Page, *Statistics of the Congressional and Presidential Election*, 15.
135. *Wood County Republican*, "Republicans Victorious on Tuesday," NOV 7, 1924.
136. Ibid., "Powell Will Head Senate," December 25, 1924.
137. Ibid., "New Superintendent Named," September 17, 1925.
138. Ibid., "Powell Will Not Run," June 3, 1926.
139. *North Baltimore Times*, "Near Lynching," September 7, 1923.
140. *Prairie Depot Observer*, "Received Klan Letter," March 9, 1923.
141. *Bloomdale Derrick*, "Attempted Assassination," August 15, 1924.
142. *North Baltimore Times*, "Arrest School Principal in War on Ku Klux Klan," September 21, 1923.

CHAPTER 6

143. *Wood County Republican*, "Fiery Cross Is Burned by Klan."
144. Ibid., "Klan Doings in Wood County," August 14, 1924.
145. Ibid.
146. Ibid., 13 "Wood County Has 500 New Klansmen," September 1924.
147. Ibid.
148. *Bloomdale Derrick*, "Klan Held Large Meeting," August 8, 1924.
149. *Wood County Republican*, "Another Lie Nailed," August 16, 1924.
150. Ibid., "Large Cross Burned," December 27, 1923.
151. *North Baltimore Times*, "Cross Burned Before K. of C. Initiation," April 13, 1923.
152. Ibid., "Silk Flag Given School by Klan," April 6, 1923.
153. *Perrysburg Journal*, "Ku Klux Klan Gives Flag and Holy Bible to Public Schools," December 13, 1923.
154. Ibid.
155. *Wood County Republican*, "Klan Funeral Passes Through Bowling Green," April 10, 1924.
156. *North Baltimore Times*, "Klansmen Visit Grave," May 25, 1923.
157. Ibid., "Death of H.M. Jones: Funeral Sunday Largely Attended Including the K.K.K.," November 2, 1923.
158. *Wood County Republican*, "The Martyred Klansman Well Received," December 18, 1924.
159. Ibid., "Klan Visit Church," August 9, 1923.
160. *North Baltimore Times*, "K.K.K. Gives Money to Negroes," August 3, 1923.
161. *Wood County Republican*, "Wood County's First Klonklave," October 4, 1923.
162. *Wood County Democrat*, "Ku Klux Gathering," October 12, 1923.
163. *Daily Sentinel-Tribune*, "Ku Klux Klan Drew a Mammoth Crowd."
164. Ibid.
165. *Wood County Republican*, "Klan Held Mammoth Klonklave," May 8, 1924.
166. Ibid., "Wood County Klonklave," October 30, 1924.

167. Ibid.
168. Ibid., "Wood County Klan Honor William Jennings Bryan," August 6, 1925.
169. Ibid.

CHAPTER 7

170. *Prairie Depot Observer*, "Church Notes: Church of Christ," June 22, 1923.
171. Ibid., "Ku Klux Cross Burned at Church," June 29, 1923.
172. Ibid., "Pastor Resigns," July 6, 1923.
173. *Wood County Democrat*, "Rev. Cavanaugh," January 19, 1923.
174. Ibid., "Cygnet News," March 16, 1923.
175. *North Baltimore Times*, "A Striking Tribute," November 23, 1923.
176. *Wood County Republican*, "Klan Opponents Fail in Attempts to Stop Klan Meetings," August 28, 1924.
177. Ibid., "Large Klanklave Held Near Fremont," May 29, 1924.
178. Ibid., "Klan Opponents Fail in Attempts to Stop Klan Meetings."
179. Blee, *Women of the Klan*, 89.
180. *Wood County Republican*, "An Outrage of Officials," January 29, 1925.
181. *North Baltimore Times*, "K.K.K. and the Coming Elections," October 26, 1923.
182. Ibid., "Klan Gives $100 to Minister," March 23, 1923.
183. *Daily Sentinel-Tribune*, "Methodist Bishop Rebuked Klan for the Interruption," October 9, 1923.
184. Jenkins, *Steel Valley Klan*, 119.
185. Ibid., 120.
186. Ibid., 124.
187. *Wood County Republican*, "Italy vs. America," November 7, 1924.
188. Ibid.
189. Ibid.
190. Ibid.
191. Ibid.

CHAPTER 8

192. Ibid., "Del-Mar Block Destroyed by Fire," September 30, 1926.
193. Ibid., "Opera House Razed," September 30, 1926.
194. *North Baltimore Times*, [Untitled news item], November 20, 1925.
195. Ibid., "Klan Row: Getting Bitter as Charges Fly About," January 25, 1924.
196. *Wood County Democrat*, "Klan Wrangle: W.E. Cahill, Who Was Active in Klan Work in Wood County, Now Denounces Organization," January 2, 1925.
197. McVeigh, *Rise of the Ku Klux Klan*, 189.
198. Hiram Wesley Evans, as quoted in McVeigh, *Rise of the Ku Klux Klan*, 189.
199. *New York Times*, "Charges Ohio Klan Created Terrorism," March 27, 1928.
200. *Pittsburgh Press*, "Klan Ouster Hearing Will Start Dec. 12," December 9, 1928, 10.
201. *New York Times*, "The Klan's Invisible Empire Is Fading," February 21, 1923.

202. Ibid. "Political Power of Klan Dissipated," February 5, 1928.

203. Records of the Ohio Knights of the Ku Klux Klan, "The Knights of the Ku Klux Klan Are Continuing Their Fight" (flyer), Center for Archival Collections, MS 731, box 2.

204. Ibid., List of Klan officers, 1941, Center for Archival Collections, MS 731, box 2.

205. *Toledo Blade*, "Klan Leader Says He Opposes Violence," October 5, 1965, 22.

206. Jaan Kangliaski,"Klan Plans Active Summer Near Northern States' Cities," *Eugene Register-Guard*, June 7, 1965, 9-A.

207. Associated Press, "Klansmen Fight Off Demonstrators," *Spartanburg Herald-Journal*, July 5, 1977.

208. Mark Rollenhagen, "Anti-Klan Activist Says Hate Groups Not Active Here," *Toledo Blade*, May 22, 1988, A-3.

209. John Nichols, "It Wasn't Deception," *Toledo Blade*, February 26, 1989, E-1.

210. *Toledo Blade*, "Jeers, Scuffles Greet Klan," June 19, 1994, A-1, A-13.

211. Ibid., A-13.

212. Ibid., "Rally Set to Protest Demonstrator's Arrest," October 26, 1994, B-1.

213. *Workers Vanguard*, "Defend NWROC Anti-Fascist Protesters!" November 11, 1994, 5.

214. Larry P. Vellequette, "Klan Rally Protesters Maintain Innocence," *Toledo Blade*, August 27, 1994, B-11.

215. *BG Sentinel-Tribune*, "Klan Rally," June 19, 1994.

216. *Toledo Blade*, "Jeers, Scuffles Greet Klan," A-1, A-13.

217. Kim Bates and Debra Baker, "Big $$$ For Klan Rallies," *Toledo Blade*, June 21, 1994, A-1.

218. Jan Larson, "Klan Asks to Hold June 19 Rally in BG," *BG Sentinel-Tribune*, June 2, 1999.

219. Jan Larson, "Klan Brings Its Message of Hate to BG," *BG Sentinel-Tribune*, June 8, 1999.

220. Ibid.

221. Chris Miller and Debbie Rogers, "KKK Rally Spectators Will Have to Pick Sides," *BG Sentinel-Tribune*, June 17, 1999, 5.

222. Jennifer Feehan, "Klan Stages 'Pathetic' Rally in B.G.," *Toledo Blade*, June 20, 1999.

223. Jan Larson and Chris Miller, "Klan Rally Tab: $25,000," *BG Sentinel-Tribune*, June 25, 1999.

224. Maryann Gibson, "Candlelight Vigil Is Saturday Night," *Sentinel-Tribune*, June 12, 1999, 8.

225. Maryann Gibson, "Go Anywhere Except Klan Rally on June 19," *BG Sentinel-Tribune*, June 16, 1999, 11.

226. Chris Miller and Jan Larson, "Unity Day Coalition: Ignore BG Klan Rally," *BG Sentinel-Tribune*, June 4, 1999, 1.

227. Palmer, "Ku Klux Kontraction."

228. Southern Poverty Law Center, "Hate Map," retrieved from http://www.splcenter.org/get-informed/hate-map#s=OH.

229. Danae King, "After Fire, Members Update Islamic Center of Greater Toledo," *BG News*, October 21, 2013.

230. Erica Blake, "Man Pleads Guilty to 3 Counts in Islamic Center Mosque Fire," *Toledo Blade*, December 20, 2012.

231. Jennifer Feehan and John Wagner, "Racist Graffiti Found at Home of BGSU Basketball Coach," *Toledo Blade*, October 16, 2012.

232. *Toledo Blade*, "BG Police Investigating 2nd Incident of Racist Vandalism," October 16, 2012.

233. Eric Lagatta and Max Filby, "BGSU Responds to 'Racially Charged' Tweets from Students," *BG News*, April 5, 2013, retrieved from http://www.bgnews.com/campus/bgsu-responds-to-racially-charged-tweets-from-students/article_992663ba-9e31-11e2-bfb2-001a4bcf887a.html.

234. Bowling Green State University, "Not in Our Town," retrieved from http://www2.bgsu.edu/notinourtown.

BIBLIOGRAPHY

PRIMARY SOURCES

Akron Beacon Journal, 1923.
Associated Press. "Klansmen Fight Off Demonstrators." *Spartanburg Herald-Journal*, July 5, 1977.
BG News, 2012–13.
Black and Gold. High school yearbook. Perrysburg High School, 1928.
Blake Tyson Collection. Center for Archival Collections, MS 311.
Bloomdale Derrick, 1923–25.
Bowling Green City Directory. Columbus, OH: Mullin-Kille, 1927.
Bowling Green Key. College yearbook. Bowling Green, OH: Bowling Green Normal College, 1923, 1924, 1927, 1930, 1934.
Bowling Green Sentinel-Tribune, 1994–99.
Bradner Advocate, 1923–26.
The Church of Rome in American Politics: Making America Catholic (anonymous author). Aurora, MO: Menace Publishing Company, 1911.
Cincinnati Board of Education. Board Minutes, February 11, 1918. Book 31. Cincinnati Board of Education Treasurer's Office, Cincinnati, OH.
Cleveland Plain Dealer, 1921–23.
Columbus Dispatch, 1922–25.
Daily Sentinel-Tribune, 1921–42, 1994–99.
Eugene Register-Guard, 1965.
Farm Journal Rural Directory of Wood County, Ohio. Philadelphia: Wilmer Atkinson Company, 1916.
Grand Rapids Tri-County News, 1923-28.

Hi-Echo. High school yearbook. Bowling Green, OH: Bowling Green High School, 1923.

Irven I. Freyman Collection. Center for Archival Collections, MS 91.

Ku Klux Klan, Inc. *America for Americans*. Atlanta, GA: Knights of the Ku Klux Klan, 1922.

————. *Should the Holy Bible Be Hidden from the Youth of America?* Atlanta, GA: Knights of the Ku Klux Klan, 1922.

Literary Digest. "For and Against the Ku Klux Klan." September 24, 1921.

Luckey Herald, 1923.

Max Shafer Collection. Center for Archival Collections, MS 336.

New York Times. "Klan Candidates Swept Ohio Cities." November 8, 1923

North Baltimore Times, 1923–26.

Ohio Federation of Churches. *Ohio Rural Church Survey 1921–22: Reports of Churches and Communities in the 88 Counties of Ohio*. Columbus, OH: Ohio Federation of Churches, 1922.

Oracle. High school yearbook. Perrysburg, OH: Perrysburg High School, 1921.

Page, William Tyler (clerk of U.S. House of Representatives). *Statistics of the Congressional and Presidential Election of November 4, 1924*. Washington, D.C.: U.S. Government Printing Office, 1925.

Paul Schmitz Collection. Center for Archival Collections, MS 617.

Perrysburg Journal, 1920–28.

Pittsburgh Press, 1928.

Records of Ohio Knights of the Ku Klux Klan, Wood County (Ohio) Chapter. Center for Archival Collections, MS 731, boxes 1–3.

Roy B. Leedy Collection. Center for Archival Collections, MS 802.

Toledo Blade, 1994–99.

Toledo News-Bee, 1921–28.

U.S. census 1930. Enumeration district 87: 1–52.

U.S. census 1920. Enumeration districts 143–79, 181, 182, 184.

U.S. census 1920. Toledo, Ohio Ward 6, District 0076, sheet 5A.

Wood County Democrat, 1922–29.

Wood County Republican, 1921–42.

Workers Vanguard. "Defend NWROC Anti-Fascist Protesters!" November 11, 1994.

SECONDARY SOURCES

Alexander, Charles C. "Kleagles and Cash: The Ku Klux Klan as a Business Organization, 1919–1930." *Business History Review* 39 (Autumn 1965): 348–67.

————. *The Ku Klux Klan in the Southwest*. Norman: University of Oklahoma Press, 1995.

Annie E. Casey Foundation. *The Changing Child Population of the United States*. Baltimore, MD: Annie E. Casey Foundation, 2011.

Blee, Katherine. *Women of the Ku Klux Klan: Racism and Gender in the 1920s*. Berkeley: University of California Press, 1991.

Boltz, Thomas W. *North Baltimore and Its Neighbors*. Charleston, SC: Arcadia Publishing, 2009.

BIBLIOGRAPHY

Bowling Green State University. "Enrollment History." Bowling Green, OH: Bowling Green State University. Retrieved from http://www.bgsu.edu/downloads/lib/file62715.pdf.

———. "Not in Our Town." Retrieved from http://www2.bgsu.edu/notinourtown/.

Boyd, Robert C. *Perrysburg Historic Architecture*. Charleston, SC: Arcadia Publishing, 2005.

Bullard, Sarah, ed. *The Ku Klux Klan: A History of Racism and Violence*. Montgomery, AL: Southern Poverty Law Center, 1991.

Chalmers, David Mark. *Hooded Americanism: The History of the Ku Klux Klan*. Durham, NC: Duke University Press, 1987.

Danford, Ardath Anne. *The Perrysburg Story, 1816–1966*. Perrysburg, OH: Sesquicentennial Publication Committee, 1966.

Dinnerstein, Leonard. *The Leo Frank Case*. Athens: University of Georgia Press, 2008.

Enders, Calvin. "Under Grand Haven's White Sheets." *Michigan Historical Review* 19, no. 1 (Spring 1993): 47–61.

———. "White Sheets in Mecosta: The Anatomy of a Michigan Klan." *Michigan Historical Review* 14, no. 2 (Fall 1988): 59–84.

Fogelson, Robert M., and Richard E. Rubenstein, eds. *Hearings on the Ku Klux Klan, 1921*. New York: Arno Press, 1969.

Fox, Craig. *Everyday Klansfolk: White Protestant Life and the KKK in 1920s Michigan*. Lansing: Michigan State University Press, 2011.

Gerlach, Larry. *Blazing Crosses in Zion: The Ku Klux Klan in Utah*. Logan: Utah State University Press, 1982.

Greenapple, H.R. *D.C. Stephenson Irvington 0492: The Demise of the Grand Dragon of the Indiana Ku Klux Klan*. Plainfield, IN: SGS Publications, 1989.

Helwig, Richard M., ed. *Wood County*. Galena: Center for Ghost Town Research in Ohio, 1990.

Honnefer, Frederick N. *Images of America: Bowling Green*. Charleston, SC: Arcadia Publishing, 2004.

Horowitz, David A., ed. *Inside the Klavern: The Secret History of a Ku Klux Klan of the 1920s*. Carbondale: Southern Illinois University Press, 1999.

———. "The Ku Klux Klan in LaGrande, Oregon." In *The Invisible Empire in the West*. Edited by Shawn Lay. Urbana: University of Illinois Press, 1992.

Howson, Embrey Bernard. *The Ku Klux Klan in Ohio After World War I* (doctoral dissertation). Columbus, OH: Ohio State University, 1951.

Jackson, Kenneth T. *The Ku Klux Klan in the City, 1915–1930*. New York: Oxford University Press, 1992.

Jenkins, William D. *Steel Valley Klan: The Ku Klux Klan in Ohio's Mahoning Valley*. Kent, OH: Kent State University Press, 1990.

Kern, Kevin F., and Gregory S. Wilson. *Ohio: A History of the Buckeye State*. Hoboken, NJ: John Wiley & Sons, 2013.

Lay, Shawn. *Hooded Knights on the Niagara: The Ku Klux Klan in Buffalo, New York*. New York: New York University Press, 1995.

Lester, John C. *Ku Klux Klan: Its Origin, Growth and Disbandment*. New York: Neale Publishing Company, 1905.

Lutholtz, William M. *Grand Dragon: D.C. Stephenson and the Ku Klux Klan in Indiana*. West Lafayette, IN: Purdue University Press, 1991.

MacLean, Nancy K. *Behind the Mask of Chivalry: The Making of the Second Ku Klux Klan*. Oxford University Press, 1995.

Martinez, James Michael. *Carpetbaggers, Cavalry, and the Ku Klux Klan: Exposing the Invisible Empire During Reconstruction*. Rowman & Littlefield, 2007.

McVeigh, Rory. "Power Devaluation, the Ku Klux Klan, and the Democratic Convention of 1924." *Sociological Forum* 16 (2001): 1–31.

———. *The Rise of the Ku Klux Klan: Right-Wing Movements and National Politics*. Minneapolis: University of Minnesota Press, 2009.

———. "Structural Incentives for Conservative Mobilization: Power Devaluation and the Rise of the Ku Klux Klan 1915-1925." *Social Forces* 77, no. 4 (1999): 1461–1496.

Meadows, Cathy J., ed. *A History of Lake Township Wood County, Ohio*. Ada, OH: Ada Herald, 1998.

Mecklin, John. *The Ku Klux Klan: A Study of the American Mind*. New York: Harcourt Brace, 1924.

Messer-Kruse, Timothy. "Memories of the Ku Klux Klan Honorary Society at the University of Wisconsin." *Journal of Blacks in Higher Education* 23 (Spring 1999): 83–93.

Moore, Leonard J. *Citizen Klansmen: The Ku Klux Klan in Indiana, 1921–1928*. Chapel Hill: University of North Carolina Press, 1997.

Ohio Department of Agriculture, Office of Farmland Preservation. *2012 Annual Report*. Reynoldsburg: Ohio Department of Agriculture, 2012. Retrieved from http://www.agri.ohio.gov/divs/FarmLand/docs/2012%20Farmland%20 Annual%20Report%20(5)_2012_08_01.pdf.

Palmer, Brian. "Ku Klux Kontraction." *Slate*, March 8, 2012.

Quarles, Chester L. *The Ku Klux Klan and Related American Racialist and Antisemitic Organizations: A History and Analysis*. Jefferson, NC: McFarland, 1999.

Safianow, Allen. "'You Can't Burn History': Getting Right with the Klan in Noblesville, Indiana." *Indiana Magazine of History* 100, no. 2 (2004): 109–54.

Sims, Patsy. *The Klan*. Lexington: University of Kentucky Press, 1996.

Southern Poverty Law Center. "Hate Map." Montgomery, AL: Southern Poverty Law Center, 2014. Retrieved from http://www.splcenter.org/get-informed/hate-map#s=OH.

Tucker, Richard. *The Dragon and the Cross: The Rise and Fall of the Ku Klux Klan in Middle America*. Hampden, CT: Archon Books, 1991.

U.S. Census Bureau. Wood County, Ohio. Washington, D.C.: U.S. Government Printing Office. Retrieved from http://quickfacts.census.gov/qfd/states/39/39173.html.

USDA National Agricultural Statistics Service. *2012 Ohio County Estimates*. Washington, D.C.: U.S. Government Printing Office, 2012. Retrieved from http://www.nass.usda.gov/Statistics_by_State/Ohio/Publications/County_Estimates/index.asp.

———. *Wood County Profile*. Washington, D.C.: U.S. Government Printing Office, 2012. Retrieved from http://www.agcensus.usda.gov/Publications/2007/Online_Highlights/County_Profiles/Ohio/cp39173.pdf.

U.S. House of Representatives. *The Ku-Klux Klan: Hearings before the Committee on Rules.* Washington, D.C.: U.S. Government Printing Office, 1921.

Van Tassel, Charles Sumner. *The First One Hundred Years of Bowling Green, Ohio.* Bowling Green: Wood County Chapter of the Ohio Genealogical Society, 1983.

Wade, Wyn Craig. *The Fiery Cross: The Ku Klux Klan in America.* New York: Oxford University Press, 1998.

Warren, G.F. "The Agricultural Depression." *Quarterly Journal of Economics* 38, no. 2 (February 1924): 183–213.

White. O.S. *North Baltimore Illustrated: The Industrial City of the Gas and Oil Districts of Wood County, Ohio.* North Baltimore, OH: North Baltimore Beacon, 1895.

Wood County Board of Education. *History and Government of Wood County, Ohio: Sesquicentennial 1803–1953.* Bowling Green, OH: Wood County Board of Education, 1953.

Wood County Commissioners. "A Guide to Wood County Government." Bowling Green, OH, 2014.

INDEX

ABOUT THE AUTHOR

D r. Michael Brooks is a historian who teaches at Bowling Green State University in Bowling Green, Ohio. He earned his BA, MA and PhD in various subfields of history. Brooks has research interests in a wide range of historical topics, and he has researched the American white supremacist and neo-Nazi movements for many years. Prior to joining BGSU as a faculty member, Brooks taught at a number of regional colleges and universities, including Wayne State University, Lourdes University and the University of Toledo. In previous careers, he worked as a journalist and as a restaurant owner, and he lives in Toledo, Ohio, with his wife, dogs and any of his adult children and grandchildren who happen to be staying for a visit.